ROCK BOTTOM

ROCK BOTTOM
PAUL MERSON

WITH HARRY HARRIS

WITH A CHAPTER BY
LORRAINE MERSON

UPDATED EDITION

BLOOMSBURY

I would like to dedicate this book to my loving wife Lorraine and my three lovely boys, Charlie, Ben and Sam.

I would like to thank the following people for all the love and support they gave me through what was a very difficult time in my life: my mum and dad, June and Fred; my brothers and sister, Keith, Gary and Louise; Lorraine's parents, Margaret and Stan, and her brother, Stephen; Uncle John and Auntie Lyn and all my family; our close friends Elaine and Neil; our sponsors, Steve and Mandy; my counsellor, Steve Stephens; my psychiatrist, Dr Tate; everyone at the FA and Arsenal Football Club; George Graham; Richard Dawes; Harry Harris and everyone else who helped me.

First published in Great Britain 1995

This paperback edition published 1996

Bloomsbury Publishing Plc, 2 Soho Square, London W1V 6HB

A CIP catalogue record for this book is available from the British Library

ISBN 0 7475 2643 5

10 9 8 7 6 5 4 3 2 1

Typeset by Hewer Text Composition Services, Edinburgh
Printed by Cox & Wyman Ltd, Reading

CONTENTS

FOREWORD by Stephen Stephens   1

1 FINDING MY FEET   11

2 FOOTBALL IN THE BLOOD   20

3 WELCOME TO THE BIG TIME   28

4 . . . AND YOU LOSE SOME   36

5 GAMBLING WITH EVERYTHING   46

6 OPENING UP   63

7 A NEW BEGINNING   88

8 ONE DAY AT A TIME   124

   AFTERWORD by Stephen Stephens   143

   LIVING WITH PAUL MERSON'S ADDICTIONS   149
   by Lorraine Merson

   UPDATE – THE 1995/6 SEASON   187

FOREWORD

by Paul Merson's counsellor, Stephen Stephens, STB, CAC
Addictions Unit Director, Marchwood Priory Hospital, Southampton

I was very honoured when Paul Merson invited me to write the foreword for this book. I have known Paul a relatively short time but during that period I have gained a unique and rare insight into his life and experience. He is a man that I consider it a privilege to know and one whom I now regard as a valued and dear friend.

I first met Paul in December 1994, in the office of Dr Austin Tate, the medical director of Marchwood Priory Hospital. My first impression was of a striking-looking young man who seemed to be rather sad. He was not at all as I had imagined him to be from the television and news pictures I had seen.

Paul had spent the previous hour or so talking to Dr Tate about entering the hospital to be treated for an addictive illness that was threatening his future in football. He had decided to accept treatment and it was now down to me to discuss with Paul the exact nature of the treatment programme that he was about to enter and the restrictions it would place on him.

It is sometimes very hard to kick a person when he is down and it was obvious to me that Paul was very down at that time. His only request was that he be allowed home for Christmas. I told him that we would not accept him for treatment if he placed conditions on it beforehand. He stated that unless he could go home for Christmas he was unable to stay for treatment. I answered by informing him that in that case then he would have to leave.

It is a terrible thing to have to do to someone when you know that he feels his life has fallen apart but it is essential to establish very clear guidelines when dealing with addictions. Addictive illness is no respecter of people of status. It doesn't matter whether you are a football star or a fishmonger, a politician or policeman, there is no immunity. Addictive illnesses affect about ten per cent of the population. It is my belief that those who are prone to such illnesses will eventually need to seek help.

Some people say that these illnesses are to do with family upbringing, or poverty, or affluence, or emotional traumas. I disagree. There are many people who have been deprived when growing up, or abused, or have faced terrible traumas, who do not go on to develop addictions. Many experts claim that addiction comes from genetic predisposition and this may well be the case. The fact is we don't really know why some people become addicts and others don't. It is probably due to a variety of factors. I don't really think that it is as important to know why addiction happens as it is to know what to do about it when it does. Knowing why is a bit like saying we lost the game last Saturday because it was windy or the defence was poor. It doesn't alter the fact that the game was lost, nor is it any consolation to the members of the team. The only value that this kind of understanding has is to help the team to change and adapt to those kind of conditions in the future. There is no point in blaming the weather. The same is true of addiction – there is no point in blaming the past or the person.

Those suffering from addictive illnesses, like a defeated football team, need a new game plan. If a plan is not developed then it is impossible to adapt to the new conditions that must be faced. In football that means losing a game. In addiction that often means gradually losing everything that is important and sadly in many cases eventually results in losing a life.

I have often watched good team managers giving interviews after a football match. The great managers recognize that even the best teams can be beaten. They also know how to accept defeat themselves and learn from it. They learn about the strengths and weaknesses of their own team and the opposition. They learn to play to their strengths and respect their weaknesses. They learn to respect the limits of what is or is not possible. And they develop a game plan which respects the opposition and still allows the team to play to its strengths.

It was to be our task at the hospital to develop a game plan with Paul which would do just the same. The vital difference was that this plan was not for a football match but for the life of a young man.

Over the weeks Paul spent at the hospital he would be working with his doctors, counsellors and nurses as well as with a number of other people, to develop a plan for life that would recognize his strengths and weaknesses. A plan enabling him to reorganize his life in a way that prevented his addictive illness from affecting him destructively.

Perhaps, in attempting to understand addiction, it is important to realize what the term means. It is my conviction that addiction can quite simply be explained by the loss of ability to predict accurately and regularly what will happen when the individual engages in certain activities. For someone with alcoholism it is not necessarily being drunk all the time – it is being unable to predict on a regular basis that they will not get drunk once they start drinking. People with alcoholism often find that they cannot guarantee their behaviour will not become a source of embarrassment to themselves or others. It is the unpredictability of drunkenness and drunken behaviour that diagnoses the addiction. Addiction is typified by periodic loss of control. Usually, as it gets worse, those periods of loss of control increase, but that can take many years.

Most people who enter treatment for any form of addiction do not believe that they are ill – they tend to believe that they are failures or bad people. Paul was not significantly different, for as he entered treatment he was confused, hurt and deeply ashamed.

He had attended a self-help group, and had been told that he needed to 'get honest'. This resulted in him telling his story to a national newspaper and with that his world collapsed. There had been headlines about cocaine, suspension from playing and, to cap it all, he had been transported from his home to a hospital in Hampshire that he knew nothing about. It is hard to believe in that situation that honesty is the best policy. However, Paul had discovered a principle that he never gave up. Throughout his treatment he remained ruthlessly honest with himself and the other members of his group. In the next few days he was to embark on a personal journey that was to change his life.

First Paul was to meet the other counsellors and members of his group. It was with them that he would explore his illness and seek the resources he would need to begin his journey to recovery. It would be these strangers who would become the key to his dealing with his deep-felt shame and guilt. It would be through the mutual trust that was to develop between them that he would begin to find the strength to begin his life anew. It was through his group, as it is for many others suffering from similar illnesses, that Paul began to find the inspiration to believe that there was a way out. To them much credit must be given. It was among people who shared the same or similar illnesses that Paul would come to understand his own, and begin to develop a daily programme through which he could live his life fully and effectively once again.

Paul's first task was to understand the exact nature of his illness. He had arrived at the hospital because he had admitted using cocaine. But was that the problem or just a symptom? As Paul began to explore his addiction it became obvious to those working with him that he was an addict.

It also became obvious that his primary drug of choice was not cocaine but alcohol. It seemed apparent that if he addressed the alcohol issue the cocaine issue would be addressed also. Paul also acknowledged that he was a compulsive gambler. He had recognized that his life was out of control and that, try as he might, he had been unable to make any kind of impact on the problems affecting him.

Over the first week Paul began to look at addiction in a new light. He realized that suffering from addiction to gambling or alcohol, or anything else for that matter, was not so much a matter of how often a person did certain things, but was more to do with the effect that these actions had on that individual's life.

Paul began to explore his addictions in depth. He could see clearly that his drinking and gambling were out of control and that this had resulted in behaviour that was a source of distress to both himself and his family. Slowly he began to explore the origins of his addictive illness. He identified its gradual progression from the behaviour of a young man just having fun to the time when he actually began to realize that something was wrong. He began to see that gradually, over the years, his behaviour had changed as his addiction had developed. He saw that he had adopted a lifestyle that attempted to cover up and hide the degree to which his life had fallen apart. He noted that over the years he had hidden the truth from his family, but also from himself.

It is a devastating thing to have to look at these aspects of your life in such close detail. In treatment Paul went through the process of taking a close look at his addiction. He wrote down each significant event as he remembered it. He recorded how he'd felt about himself on each occasion. Then he had to find the courage to share this information with his counsellors and group. He completed this task about a week before Christmas, far earlier than I had expected, and I was able to tell him that he would probably be eligible for a weekend leave. As Christmas fell on a weekend he would be able to join his wife and two children for that day.

Paul fully realized that he was powerless over alcohol, gambling and drugs, and that his life had become chaotic and unmanageable. He now knew the full extent of his problems. He fully accepted that he could never successfully use alcohol, drugs or gamble again. He recognized that each of these issues could and had wrecked his life. He realized that through his illness he had been instrumental in hurting people that he loved, and had put his life and career at risk. He had a major problem.

As Paul shared this stage of his treatment with us I recall that he felt a mixture of deep sadness, regret and relief. The sadness and tears were not for himself but for those people he felt that he had hurt, particularly his parents, wife and children. He also felt sad for the many people who had helped him and for the example he may have set for others. The relief came from recognizing that he was not bad but ill. It became apparent to him that, try as he might, he could not have done better until he was given the tools to do so. He realized that the strength of will that had given him the determination and commitment to make it to the top in football and to play for England was not enough for him to overcome his addiction. Paul had learned a vital lesson – that he could be and was defeated. Through looking at his own experience, he had discovered that he had to abstain from alcohol and drugs. He realized that he could no longer take the risk of gambling. He recognized that he would have to make enormous changes to his lifestyle if he were to succeed. Most importantly, he realized that he could not do it alone. Paul had problems – he knew that – but he also knew that he had to take these problems seriously if he was not to risk losing everything he had.

Paul was suffering from an illness that causes the death of thousands of people each year. An illness that results in the break-up of marriages, loss of jobs, imprisonment and crime. An illness which does not usually make itself obvious for many years but results in feelings of terrible shame and failure even though many sufferers hold down highly successful jobs. An illness which locks people into their own personal hell from which, sadly, very few find a way of escape. When Paul had completed the first stage of his treatment he knew how difficult his problems were to overcome. This phase of treatment is always very painful to go through. It is a highly emotional phase and Paul, like many others, experienced deep grief and sorrow at this time. He was ruthless with himself, often stating that he didn't ever want to have to repeat treatment and was not going to leave any stones unturned in his life. Looking at his life made the evidence of the problem obvious. By coming into hospital he had acknowledged that something was wrong but the solutions were outside his experience; for these he would have to rely on other people to a very large extent.

When most people are ill they go to the doctor and are usually prescribed a course of medication or surgery. When someone with an addiction is ill their medicine is other people. When Paul wanted to know whether it was possible to begin recovering from his illness the best evidence was to be found among those people who were themselves recovering.

With this goal in mind Paul met groups of people suffering and recovering from alcohol and drug problems as well as attending his two group therapy sessions per day. He learned from their experiences as well as from his individual sessions with me, Dr Tate and the other counselling staff. He began to realize that recovery was possible. He began to develop new coping techniques. He realized that by talking to others and adopting a specific plan of action he could gain a daily reprieve from his illness.

Paul made decisions to adopt a new way of life which could free him to be himself and enjoy the things that were important to him. He used a diary to record and review the events of each day. He began his day with a pause for thought and reflection about himself and the frame of mind he was in. He learned to accept the things he couldn't change and to change the things he could. At each stage of this process he used his group as a resource to give him feedback on each new strategy. It was only with their endorsement that he incorporated these plans into his life.

The last stage of Paul's treatment at the hospital involved his taking a thorough look at his life from his birth to the present. This, like all the previous processes, he wrote down and then shared with his group and counsellors. The purpose of this was to help Paul to accept himself totally, with both his strengths and his weaknesses. To help Paul to accept his humanity and frailty. To help him realize that it is all right to not be perfect and that good is good enough.

As Paul shared his life story some events struck me that I

would like to record. Paul spoke of his childhood and of a father who saw Paul's footballing ability. He spoke of going to football matches each week and playing football with his dad. He spoke of his mother, who was there for him. He painted a picture of a real family that had problems and joys of their own but managed to give him the drive, skill and support to go on to become a professional footballer. He spoke of his parents and brothers and sister with gratitude and affection. He spoke of his own family, and particularly his wife, expressing deep gratitude for the loyalty and love she had shown him when he was incapable of being loving himself. He spoke of the gratitude he felt towards his club, and particularly Mr Friar, for the support both he and they had provided. He spoke of his desire to play football again and to help others who suffered from his illness. He spoke as a young man who had discovered a real sense of his own identity and value.

When the time for Paul to leave treatment was imminent Dr Tate and I met representatives of the Football Association. They knew that the media would be highly interested in Paul and his future. After discussions about Paul's ongoing needs it was decided with his club that it would be in everyone's best interests to call a press conference to coincide with Paul's departure from the hospital. The FA were to inform me when and where this conference was to occur. I travelled with Paul to the conference and stayed with him before it took place. I stood in the room as the cameras rolled and flashed. I saw what seemed to be a hundred cameras all flash at once as Paul broke down in tears. I sat with him after it was over and drove back to his home with him that evening before returning to Southampton later that night. Many people will recall those events. The conference seemed to release the pain and anguish of the past two months and bring to a close a chapter which had begun with an article in the national press. I thought it was appropriate.

Paul's treatment some months ago was not intended to cure his addiction. In fact it is based on the conviction that addictions cannot be cured, but can only be arrested or managed.

Paul is leading an alcohol and drugs-free life today. Paul does not gamble today. Yet he knows that this is just the beginning. He knows that unless he accepts responsibility for his illness each day it could affect him again. He knows that he must use the support of those who share his illness with him. From speaking with Paul it is clear that he recognizes that his recovery is something that he cannot take for granted. He realizes that recovery demands a great deal of effort if he is to retain the benefits it has to offer.

I went to watch Paul play his first match after returning to the game; it was against AC Milan at Highbury. We had agreed that I should arrive at the ground at 6.45 p.m. and spend sometime with Paul before the game. As it happened I arrived at 7.45, about ten minutes before the kick-off, having been stuck in traffic. On arrival I was taken to see Paul by the club physiotherapist. Paul entered the room looking healthy and calm. I asked him how he was. He confirmed that he felt relaxed. He asked the same question of me and I had to admit that I was rather agitated as a result of my late arrival. At that moment I began to wonder which of us was the counsellor and which was the patient!

I sat through the game waiting with anticipation until halfway through the second half. I heard the chants of 'Merson, Merson' and 'Bring on Merson'. I heard the roar of the fans as the substitution was made. I felt a personal sense of pride that somehow the staff of our hospital had contributed to that moment. I thought of the pride his parents must have felt to have contributed to so many such moments. I thought of the pressure that a vulnerable young man was facing. I thought of so many people I have met who have made the same journey as Paul and begun to rediscover their lives and value. I thought of those who did not get the opportunity or were incapable of grasping it. For me it was quite a moment.

After the game I met Paul's parents and family. They seemed so proud of him.

I wish Paul every success with this book, his career and the rest of his life. I hope that he will always be able to take each day as it comes and remember that the game isn't over until the final whistle blows.

S.D. Stephens, 23 April 1995

1

FINDING MY FEET

My grandfather on my dad's side was a coalman; so was my dad. They were both gamblers, and my other grandad liked a drink or two. In many ways my life has mirrored my dad's. But I don't blame him, or either of my grandads, for the problems I have faced.

I'm often asked why it all happened to me. Of course, there will always be some who will point the finger at my family and say, 'like father, like son'. Well, I can tell them now – forget it. I love my dad and I loved my grandads when they were alive. I don't point the finger at any of them; I point it straight at myself. I don't believe my addictions are hereditary. I'm the one responsible, and it's down to me to put my life right after overcoming my problems with gambling, drink and drugs.

Stephen Stephens, my counsellor at Marchwood Priory Hospital, which was where I received six weeks' life-changing treatment, has become a close friend and trusted adviser. I talk to him on the phone two or three times a week. He has advised me, as part of my therapy, to be open and truthful about all matters, but particularly about my upbringing and how that has affected me in the long term.

Part of my rehabilitation was to share my life story in group therapy. I had to be completely honest about it, but naturally I couldn't recall everything that had happened to me in my early life. It was a stressful time. In reality, a lot of what happened to me in the past is still very much a blur. On the other hand, the way forward seems much clearer as I fight my addictions day by day.

If it wasn't for my mum, June, and my dad, Fred, I don't believe I'd be a footballer today. I owe them for all the hard work they have done for me – in my early footballing days they took me all over the place to play and pushed me when I didn't fancy it. I'm grateful too for everything they've done for my brothers and sisters. They live in Northolt, north-west London; it was the second home we lived in and it's very important to me. My younger brothers, Gary, twenty, and Keith, twenty-two, still live there with my sister, Louise.

The Mersons are a close-knit family. And a large one. My dad is one of thirteen children, and has six brothers and six sisters. There are forty-two grandchildren, fifty-three great-grandchildren and who knows how many great-great-grandchildren. Christmas is a hectic day. Everyone arrives in shifts at my nan's (my dad's mother) house and when I was a kid I used to love going over there on Christmas morning.

Nan – eighty-seven years of age, bless her – lives in Dollis Hill, not far from Northolt. She is of Italian descent, and her grandfather was called Daytono Valvona. They came from Venice. I always said I would play for Italy! Nan's name is Dorothy, and everyone in the family calls her 'Dolly'. But my little boys, Charlie, four, and Ben, two, have always called her 'Nanny Dolphin'.

Dad's father was christened Charles but always known as 'Chick'. He died in September 1990 and my first-born arrived in December the same year. We were going to call him Luke, but eventually we decided on Charlie, after my grandad. I was very upset when grandad died, and his funeral was a very sad family occasion. I knew him very well. He was a funny old bloke, who never went out of the house. When I married Lorraine he didn't come to the wedding as he wasn't well, although he didn't like going out anyway. Every Saturday you'd find him in his favourite chair in the living room watching the racing on the television. He loved a bet on the horses, but he never touched a drink in his life.

My grandmother on my mother's side was called Megan, but

known as 'Cis' to the family. She died of bowel cancer at the age of fifty-eight, when I was five years old, and I've hardly any recollection of her. All I can recall is her Dame Edna-style painted glasses.

She and my grandad Bert lived near us in Stonebridge. Bert was eighty-two when he died, two years ago. I'll always remember how he enjoyed a good laugh. He was a man who always saw the funny side of life, and who liked a sing-song and a few drinks. But my brothers and I were scared stiff whenever he stayed at our house. He had this terrifying habit off nodding off to sleep with a lighted fag in his mouth or in his hand. We were never able to sleep a wink until we had stayed up to watch that fag go out, and this went on until I was seventeen.

Bert was a French-polisher. The best. He worked on the longest bank counter in London, and one day I went to the bank to watch him. He owned his own business, Morgan and Haynes, in Willesden. By the time he died, I had moved out of the family home but he remained very close to Keith and Gary, who carried on living with my parents.

We are a poor family, with not much real money around and certainly none of the trappings of wealth, even though I have earned quite a bit as a top-ranked football star. It has mostly been gambled away.

Life began for me at 3.30 a.m. on 20 March 1968, at the Central Middlesex Hospital in Park Royal. My mum tells me that I was twelve days overdue and that she went into hospital originally because the doctors thought she had gone into labour. In fact she had a kidney infection. When I arrived I had wispy blond hair with a little quiff – and I'm just the same now!

My mum has told me that I fell very ill when I was just six months old. I woke up one morning as right as rain, had my breakfast, but then turned cold. Mum put me to bed but within an hour or so I was very sick. When she picked me up I was like a rag doll. Dad's sister, who lived with us at that time with her family, called the doctor out. He told her that if my breathing deteriorated and became any faster, they should call him back.

But my auntie wouldn't have any of it. She felt I should be in hospital and told the doctor.

My mum wrapped me in a blanket, and she has told me how pitiful I looked. Dad turned up after work and when he saw me he cried his eyes out. When they got me to hospital I was grey, eyes black, mouth blue. They thought I had meningitis, and gave me dozens of tests; they even took swabs from the nose and throat of both mum and dad. They put a penicillin drip in my head. It was frightening for my parents, because they thought they were going to lose me. I came through it, of course, because here I am.

Before we settled in Northolt when I was ten, I was brought up in a top-floor flat in a large Victorian house in Sellons Avenue, Harlesden, further into London. We had a kitchen-cum-dining-room, one bedroom and a living room. We lived with my dad's sister Maureen, her husband Frank and their three children.

Like other boys, I got into scraps and my share of trouble every now and then. But as I got older football started to take a grip on me, and I would kick a ball about in our flat. This annoyed intensely the old lady in the flat below, who would bang on her ceiling with her broom to try to keep us quiet. But it never worked. She would come marching up the stairs, bang on our door, and my dad would answer it. 'Mr Merson, would you like to come downstairs for a moment,' she would say. She would take my dad over to her piano. Then she would tell him to look at the amount of dust and debris that had accumulated on it from the disturbance that had been taking place on the floor above.

My pals were Michael Kleen, who lived next door, and Noland, from across the road. We hung about with my two cousins, Billy and 'Toto'. As soon as I was able to kick a ball I was out in the street with my pals and cousins. We were always playing football. We lived on a dangerous bend but we never cared, and even played cricket up against the lamppost. When I was a little older I went over to the park and found myself playing football with older boys. I never seemed to play with kids of my own age.

My dad would take me to the park every night when I came

home from school, before he went out to play cards. I loved it. He would give me plenty of advice. 'Don't pick up the ball . . . take your hands off your hips.' The Arsenal coaches are still telling me to take my hands off my hips!

My dad didn't drink very much, a pint of pale ale now and again, but he did gamble, and he loved to play cards. So he was always in need of money to gamble with. My mum worked as a cleaner at Remploy, Staples Corner, and earned £16 a week, which she would hide away so my dad couldn't get his hands on it and lose it playing cards. Dad would tuck me under the bed to find out where my mum hid her wages, offering me a treat for the information.

My mum was in hospital for six weeks having Gary and my dad had lost his job as he had to stay at home and look after me. They gave him a pay-off, and my mum hid the money as usual, telling him that they needed it to pay the bills. But my dad told me to get under the bed – I was seven at the time – to find out where my mum put the money. To me it was a game, and a lot of fun.

At times my dad was so short of money that he would take me out to the park at 7 a.m. – just to dodge the milkman because he couldn't pay his bill. I always used to wonder why he wanted to play football in the park so early in the morning.

But I thought my dad was great fun, and couldn't wait for him to take me to play football. I hated it when he went off on a Saturday morning to play football without me. His mates would turn up outside the house and a car horn would sound. I'd do my best to persuade him to stay, and cry because I didn't want him to go. It got so bad that my parents had to put me in another room before this Saturday-morning ritual in the hope that I wouldn't hear the horn and get myself in a state.

Life couldn't have been much fun for my mum. She laughs about it now, but at the time my dad's gambling was a problem. I used to beg him not to go out at night. I would say to him, 'You're not going out tonight, dad, are you?' It's funny but that's what my eldest boy, Charlie, now says to me. And now I don't go out like I used to. To me it seems unreal, that what I used to say at seven Charlie is now saying aged four when he gets home from school.

My dad would stay out most of the night and when he didn't come back my mum would get me to ring wherever the card school was taking place that particular night. I'd ask if my dad was there, and I'd be crying on the phone. It was funny how they always came back to the phone and said that I'd just missed him, because I could hear him talking in the background, saying, 'Tell him I've left.' He just couldn't put the cards down.

Mum was pregnant with Gary, so I was about six when one day dad arranged to pick me up after school. She walked round to the school and found me still waiting for him. It had never happened before and my mum could only assume that something was wrong. She was frantic, ringing all the hospitals. When my dad eventually came home, at eight o'clock that evening, she called him all the names under the sun. He'd been out playing cards and forgotten all about meeting me from school.

Dad would return from his card sessions and give my mum money. But she suspected that he might have lost and borrowed the money from a friend just so that he didn't have to turn up without a penny and find himself in big trouble again for losing everything.

You could always tell from his moods whether he had won or lost at cards, or betting. I was so excited when England scored a late goal against Scotland that I came running out of the house to tell him. He'd gone outside because he couldn't bear to watch the game any more. Having placed a bet on Scotland to win 2-0, he was so tense he couldn't watch when they were two up. I couldn't find him because he'd gone for a walk around the block, but eventually I was the bearer of the news that Mick Channon had scored a goal for England from a penalty with a minute to go. Dad was hopping mad when I told him.

I was not really a happy little boy. I suppose the constant rows between my mum and dad affected me badly. I used to wet the bed so much that I had to sleep on a plastic sheet every night. My mum told me I sucked one thumb so much that it became shorter than the other one. Apparently I didn't stop sucking my thumb until I was ten. We had a lot of mice in the house, so we kept cats, and while my brother would kick the cat down the stairs, I would suck my thumb and wet the bed. I was always a nervous little boy, frightened easily, and I think this came from hearing my mum and dad arguing.

I also had a speech impediment: I couldn't pronounce my s's. (Maybe that was an advantage if I missed a goal because I would shout '-hit'.) My mum took me to a clinic and they helped me. I also had reading difficulties, and never sat down and read a book until I was eleven. Either the school never taught me the basics of writing and reading, or I never really paid attention.

My dad played for the Queens Park Rangers youth team when he came out of the army. Jack Taylor was the manager and in goal was the England keeper Ron Springett. Dad was the quickest footballer in London over a hundred yards. Now you know where I get my pace from! But he didn't quite make it to the first team and ended up playing Saturday-afternoon football. In one match that I was watching he broke his nose, but you would have thought he had broken his neck by the amount of fuss he made about it when he got home!

I was so attached to my dad that I wanted to go to work with him every Saturday morning. I'd get all my gear ready, putting my Doc Martens boots beside the bed with old jeans and a big, warm jumper. Sometimes he wouldn't wake me and I would get very upset. But when he did I used to love going 'coaling', knocking on people's doors and shouting, 'Coalmen!'

Dad supported Arsenal, but I was a Chelsea fan. I adored Ray Wilkins. So it was the biggest thrill of my young life when my uncle Bobby got me Ray Wilkins's shirt. My uncles Bobby and Lenny worked in a bar in Marbella every summer. One year Chelsea were out there on tour. Players, liking a drink or two, frequently visited my uncles' bar, and Bobby, who was a car dealer, got chatting to Ray and told him about me. The day the team were leaving the resort of Lloret del Mar, the Chelsea star came in and threw his training shirt at Bobby and said, 'Give that to your nephew.' You can imagine how I felt when he came back with that shirt.

I'll never forget the first game I saw. I went with an older boy that my parents knew from the Crownhill Club, where we went every Saturday night. It was Chelsea at home to West Ham at Stamford Bridge, and I remember Clive Walker was in the Chelsea side. He was a player who excited me, and I couldn't wait to go back. It was quite an eventful first game – not least because my dad was nicked for parking on a zigzag line and the rival fans ended up fighting on the pitch. There was also trouble in the crowd and I got separated from my friend and ended up phoning my mum and dad from Edgware Road underground station. It gave them a real fright until they finally found me.

I enjoyed my family holidays, when we used to go to Caister holiday camp in Norfolk and stay in self-catering chalets. I went in for the Tarzan competition – holding a number ten, the number I would one day wear for Arsenal. But I didn't win anything.

I got on well with my brothers and my sister Louise. Apart, that is, from pulling her hair out when she was a baby. Of course the three of us would fight – like most brothers and sisters do – but nothing excessive and we are all good friends to this day.

As for football, I was progressing very nicely. I played for Brent Schools District under-elevens, though at nine I was a year younger than all my team-mates, and I was their leading goalscorer. For the past sixteen years my dad has proudly kept all the old newspaper cuttings about me in scrapbooks, all in perfect order. He's got a separate one covering the times I've played for England, and even one about when I was a bad boy. It's incredible how your memory can seem virtually empty, but once the family start looking at the cuttings and talking, it all comes flooding back in graphic detail.

Dad has still got the first cutting about me, when the *Evening Standard* reported my exploits with the under-elevens in my debut against Hackney, still aged nine. He was working the day I played, but he got home early and asked how I did. I told him we had won 6-1. 'Did you score?' he wanted to know. I told him I got five of the six goals. Was he thrilled!

Not everyone was deliriously happy about the number of goals I was getting. I attended Keble Memorial School from the age of five until we moved house when I was ten. Our school team was thrashing Salusbury Road by five goals at half time, and I had scored all five. Our teacher came over to me and told me not to score any more goals! He explained that I mustn't get any more because we were embarrassing the children in the rival team.

I don't recall a great deal about school, apart from the fact that I didn't like it and didn't learn very much. It was adjacent to a nunnery and we were always getting up to all sorts of mischief. One of our pranks was to jump over the fence to look at the girls.

At the age of eleven I nearly made it to Wembley.

It was a Smiths Crisps-sponsored six-a-side national schools tournament and Brent Schools District reached the semi-finals, where we faced the Essex Schools District side, which included the young Paul Ince. A place at Wembley was at stake but we lost. I can't remember how well Paul played that day. And I don't remember him kicking anyone!

What I do remember clearly from that time is that, for all his faults, my dad loved me. I loved him when I was small and I still love him today.

2

FOOTBALL IN THE BLOOD

Swapping our Dickensian existence in a flat in Harlesden for a house in Northolt changed my life completely. For a start, I stopped weeing the bed and sucking my thumb. At one time a boy who couldn't wait to get out of the house fast enough, now all I wanted to do was stay in. I'd become a recluse!

Mum and dad had the chance of a council house with four bedrooms and took it. Although we had had the whole top floor of a Victorian house in Harlesden, there was only one bedroom and at first we had shared with my aunt and uncle and their children. It was pretty crowded.

Just a year after we settled into our new home I had a nasty accident in the field at the back that could easily have damaged my leg permanently. Our house was one of the first to be built, and the estate was still under construction, with a great deal of work going on. One Friday evening in the summer, when my dad was at home watching Test cricket on TV and my mum was at work, I was playing football on the grass with a few mates. I was in goal and as I came storming out for a slide tackle a piece of metal concealed in the grass tore through my skin-tight jeans and pierced my knee to the bone. The builders must have discarded a piece of jagged metal there.

I got up, not noticing the metal had penetrated my knee, and was about to play on when I saw blood pouring from the wound. I panicked and ran straight to a neighbour's house. An ambulance was called, and off I went to hospital, where they operated, although not immediately because I'd had a drink of water about three hours earlier. The surgeon sowed up all the ligaments inside the knee. I still have the huge scar today, and at the time it was touch and go whether I would play football again. In fact the doctors were concerned whether I would even be able to bend my knee again.

We went off on holiday to a caravan site at Bracklesham Bay, in West Sussex. Naturally I had been warned to take it very easy, but you can't keep a boy of eleven still for long. I ended up playing cricket with the rest of the kids on the caravan site, but I insisted I had to be wicket-keeper and tried to keep as still as I could.

I slipped and opened up the wound. Back to hospital, this time in Chichester, for more stitches. Now I had a total of thirty inside and on the outside of my knee.

When I got back to school I sat next to a boy and for weeks I thought he stunk. But it wasn't him. It was me: the wound had became infected.

School was no longer a nightmare for me. I went to Ravenor School in nearby Greenford, where the PE teacher, John McAllister, gave me extra reading lessons. He spotted my love of sport and of football in particular, and got me to read the sports pages in the newspapers.

At the age of thirteen I saw my first England international at Wembley: the World Cup qualifier against Hungary in 1982. As we walked to the game, we spotted the England team coach and I waved to the players and they waved back. But I doubt very much that the likes of Kevin Keegan were waving at me. There must have been hundreds of kids waving at the players, and they were just returning the greeting. But as far as I was concerned, it seemed as though they were waving at me alone. Later, as I sat there watching England play, it suddenly dawned on me that I wanted to play for my country. That night I dreamed I was playing for England.

My knee recovered, and I made a lot of progress with my football. I was becoming the star of the Ealing District Schools side – so much so that the teacher would come and get me out of bed to ensure that I played. No one else from that team made it to professional level, which was a big surprise to me.

I started training at Watford, where Nigel Callaghan, Kenny Jackett and Steve Terry, the first-team stars of that time, trained schoolboys twice a week. I was recommended to Watford by Tommy Darling, who spotted me playing for my Sunday-morning team, Kingsbury's Forest United.

It was while I was playing for Forest in a Middlesex Schools Cup Final that I first got a bad attack of palpitations. It was an awful experience, as I found it impossible to catch my breath and went dizzy and had to come off. My mum was worried sick. She said that I had to get some medical help. But she also knew how nervous I was. She said that unless my nerves improved I'd end up in the nut-house. How close to the truth she was!

Arsenal's chief scout, Steve Burtenshaw, came to watch me and tried to persuade me and my parents that I should go to Highbury. He would turn up at our house and sit there for hours talking about me joining the club. Arsenal were not alone in chasing me: I also had scouts from Chelsea, West Ham and QPR asking to go training.

Finally, when I reached the age of fourteen, it came down to a straight choice between Watford and Arsenal. I had become really attached to Watford, having trained there and watched the first team on many occasions, but Arsenal were very keen. One of their scouts, Bill Groves, was so persistent I thought he was going to take up residence in our home. (After I signed, Bill and I became good friends and he and his lovely wife Rene went on holiday with my family. He is still at Highbury, in charge of the Celebrity XI.) Bill spent one evening so determined to convince my mum and dad that I should go to Arsenal that I ran upstairs crying, I was so confused.

Never one to give up, Bill then invited the whole family as the guests of the club to watch one of the Gunners' home matches against Everton. The plan was to impress us with their facilities as well as with the ability of the team. But I couldn't keep my eyes off one player – and he wasn't in the Arsenal team. All I can remember is the performance of an Everton player called Alan Biley, with his long, flowing blond hair and his sleeves rolled down over his fingers. The man had style; he caught the eye. In fact he was the only player on the field who stood out. He was the type of player I like. Perhaps he was the sort of showman I wanted to become.

Maybe it was because my dad supported Arsenal, I don't really know, but I made my mind up to sign for the Gunners. On 26 April 1982, just turned fourteen, I signed schoolboy forms for Arsenal. That is really the first big commitment to a club. Signing Associated schoolboy forms means that you cannot be linked with any other club until you leave school at the age of sixteen, and then that club has first option to retain you as an apprentice and then as a professional. You hear of boys' parents being paid inducements to sign for a club, but no offers were made to them or me. It was purely my decision, and I made it.

Now, every Monday and Thursday when I went training, I had to embark on an arduous journey that lasted twenty-one stops on the underground. My training session would take place at the Highbury gym, which in those days was a gravel surface. I hated it. Coming home afterwards, many times I was fast asleep by the time the train rattled into Northolt station and woke me up, and as many times I sailed on past my stop.

Often my dad would drive me home and that meant a stop for a Kentucky Fried Chicken supper. During the journey we would listen to David Bowie; I loved his number 'Space Oddity'.

At this stage it was not going well for me on the football front. I was just not being picked. I hardly got a kick. I never started a game and the best I could expect was ten minutes as a substitute. We played on Sunday mornings and I felt I was wasting my time. In the youth team at that time was Mickey Thomas, who made the transition to apprentice, then full-time professional, the first team and even the England side. But no one else made the grade. Worse still, it didn't look like I'd be among the ones to make it, either.

When I left school at sixteen I was small and frail, and at Arsenal they certainly thought I was too small to do well. I had talks with the chief scout, Steve Burtenshaw, followed by a chat with Don Howe, the manager. Don told me that I was really small but the club were going to offer me an apprenticeship on the off-chance that I might grow. Clearly they must have thought I had some talent worth persevering with. So in 1984 I signed on as an Arsenal apprentice.

I met Lorraine Costin in February of that year, when we were both fifteen, although I turned sixteen a month later. It was at a schoolkids' club disco called Ameretas. Too shy to make the initial approach, I spoke to Lorraine's friend and told her that I fancied her. And it developed from there.

Lorraine liked my monogrammed ring that my parents had bought me for my birthday. She asked me where I went to school and I said that I had left and that I played football with Arsenal. I thought to myself that that would surely impress her, but Lorraine has since told me that she hadn't a clue about football and so it had meant very little to her.

She couldn't have been impressed by my gear either. I was wearing jeans and trainers, and my dad's leather jacket. Given how small I was at the time, you can imagine how big that leather jacket must have looked! It felt eighteen sizes too big. Lorraine has told me that she really hated that jacket. Despite the way I must have looked, she took a shine to me, and we made arrangements to meet up again.

It wasn't until we had been going out for a while that Lorraine was told by one of my mates that I was doing very well at Arsenal as an apprentice. One Saturday I rang her up and told her that I was playing in a game and asked her along with my mum and dad. She agreed to go and that was the first time she had ever been to a game. After that she went to every game I played in.

In September, for Lorraine's sixteenth birthday, I bought her a monogrammed ring just like mine but with the initials 'L.C.'. It was the first present I ever bought her, and it had taken months to save the money out of my wages as an apprentice.

To be honest, the real reason it wasn't easy for me to save was because by then I had started betting and drinking.

I was sixteen when I first started drinking heavily. My parents could tell how bad it was, as they would see me sitting on their settee with ten empty beer bottles around me when they returned from their Saturday night out at a restaurant. So, years later, when I rang my mum from the treatment centre where I had been told I was an alcoholic, to confess the full extent of my addictions, the part about the drinking came as no surprise to her.

I started off drinking Pernod and blackcurrant in my teens, when I went out with my mates on Saturday nights. I remember that if I was sick going home afterwards it always used to make a terrible mess in the back of the cab. Since then I've probably tried just about every drink known to man.

As for gambling, the moment I left school and began earning money I was betting every penny of it. I started putting money on horses at sixteen and would spend my entire month's pay as an apprentice, £100, on betting – in just one day. I'm ashamed to say that my mum had to bail me out by giving me some of her allowance. She gave me money whenever I was short, and that was more often than not.

I once won £840 on a football accumulator bet and promised my parents that I would pay their telephone bill. But on the Monday I was back at the bookmaker's blowing the lot on the dogs and the horses. Pay the phone bill? I couldn't afford my bus fare home. I ended up borrowing a fiver from a mate to get a taxi.

My dad told me that his father had said to him that it was bad luck to bet on a Monday. 'Never bet on a Monday,' he told me. He should have said never bet on a Tuesday, Wednesday, Thursday, Friday, Saturday or Sunday either.

So I was really hooked on gambling from an early age. I loved it, I loved just sitting in the betting shops, but I didn't have a clue about the damage it was doing. All my sense of reason, of proportion, went out of the window because betting was the only thing that mattered to me.

On 1 December 1985, when I was seventeen, I signed professional forms for a four-year contract with Arsenal worth £150 a week. I thought I was a millionaire! Lorraine and I got engaged the following year and I thought that taking that step would help me settle down. I was right. Whether we went out together or just sat in watching television, Lorraine had a calming effect on me. She kept me away from bad influences, and for a while my life took on some shape.

She was really good for me, and very supportive. When she passed her driving test she would pick me up at my parents' house at 8.30 a.m. and drive me all the way to Arsenal's training ground at London Colney, in Hertfordshire. Then she would drive back to go to work. She told me she didn't want me travelling on the tube as I would have to get up at 6.30 to get to Highbury and then get on the club coach to the training ground. In this way I was able to enjoy an extra two hours' sleep.

But then I went off the rails again. Although we were engaged, I was again drinking and betting all the time, going out every night and staying out late. It was becoming a problem even in those early days.

My football was suffering. But not because of my excesses in my social life. Pat Rice was in charge of the youth team and I was just not getting a game. He never played me at the start of a game and I had had enough. I wasn't enjoying my football, and I had become frustrated sitting on the bench waiting for a few minutes at the end of the game. I was earning £30 a week but some of my mates were working as labourers on the building site and pulling in £150. I wanted to pack it all in, but my dad talked me into carrying on.

Drugs! Well, I can't pretend I never dabbled when I was a kid. I smoked dope when I was sixteen, just before I signed for Arsenal. The kids I hung around with smoked it, and it seemed the natural thing to do. The first time it made me go dizzy, my face turned yellow and my eyes bloodshot. I went home, making sure my mum and dad didn't see me, and went straight to bed. But it also relaxed me, and being a nervous kid, that was a wonderful experience for me.

I used dope quite a bit when I hung around with my mates, but afterwards I'd always feel very hungry and have to go to the twenty-four-hour service station and get some Turkish Delight. Once I became an apprentice at Arsenal, though, I stopped smoking dope straight away.

3

WELCOME TO THE BIG TIME

Insecurity, nervousness and palpitations during games were the first manifestations of problems that would develop into something far more serious. When I first started to make my way as a footballer with Arsenal I had such severe attacks of nerves that a doctor warned me that unless I cured the problem I wouldn't be able to carry on.

In one reserve match at Chelsea I had to come off because my nerves were shattered. Peter Bonetti was in goal that day. I had a great chance to score and dribbled round him, but I was struck by an attack of palpitations and caught by a defender. I suppose it was because I was a shy young lad, lacking in confidence. Even at this early stage I needed the drink to provide that confidence. The booze was an escape from my shyness, which was so bad that I couldn't handle it.

I was drinking heavily from the very start, but it didn't dawn on me then what it would do to me. But neither drink nor gambling sidetracked me from my main ambition, which was to make it to the top in football.

Suddenly my fortunes were changing on the football front. At the age of seventeen I was in the Arsenal reserves alongside such illustrious names as Pat Jennings, Tony Adams, Michael Thomas, David Rocastle, Paul Davis, Martyn Hayes and Chris Whyte. My dad has kept the team sheet from a reserve match against Crystal Palace on 30 March 1985, and all those great names from Arsenal appeared on the list. On the Palace side were Colin Hill, now captain at Leicester, David Cork, Greg Allen, a friend of mine, and Jimmy Carter, who has ended up as a team-mate at Highbury.

I made my name in a Guinness six-a-side tournament at the G-Mex Centre in Manchester. Charlie Nicholas was so impressed with this unfamiliar youngster that he described me as the new Ian Rush. Tony Gubba was the commentator for a tournament that got TV exposure and he raved about the boy for the future.

At that time Arsenal were in the market to buy a big-name striker. They tried to sign Tony Cottee and Frank McAvennie. Both deals fell through and that pushed me closer to the first team. But before I made my big breakthrough in the first team I was loaned for a month to Third Division Brentford.

I thought I had joined a pub team! The booze flowed on the team coach on the trips back from away fixtures. Some first-team stars loved a drink, and there was little pretence to the contrary. I couldn't believe it. It was some experience, and quite an eye-opener for a youngster like me.

Frank McLintock, one-time captain of Arsenal's double-winning team, was the manager for my first game for Brentford, which also turned out to be his last with the club. We had got thumped 4-1 and that was the end for poor old Frank.

As well as the players getting stuck into the lagers, the Bees' top player sat at the back of coach smoking a fag. By the time we got back to London many were paralytic. This was not exactly conducive to helping me cut down on my own drinking.

Steve Perryman took charge of the team. We went up to Bolton, where Phil Neal was the manager, and we won 2-0. Afterwards a couple of our players couldn't get out of the showers fast enough to rush off to the off-licence to fetch the beers for the journey home.

Perryman wanted to extend my loan period. I was tempted. It was certainly better playing first-team football, even with Brentford, than playing in the reserves at Arsenal. In fact, I loved my time at Brentford and I'm grateful to all the lads, who were a big help to me.

Before long I turned eighteen and George Graham had me earmarked for first-team football at Arsenal. I had grown at last, but I was still very skinny. Fortunately my game was about touch and control, not power. There was little chance of that with my skinny frame! George brought me back to Highbury and the following Saturday he made me substitute in the game against Manchester City, where I came on to make my first-team debut.

My first touch was to hit the ball straight into the North Bank. What a start!

We won 3-0 but I didn't play again until five matches before the end of the season. The boss picked me to go to Wimbledon when they used to play at Plough Lane. In that game, my full de-but, I scored. It was a header that Lawrie Sanchez tried to keep out with his hand, but he couldn't stop it going in. We won 2-1, but I could easily have scored half a dozen. Funnily enough, I seemed to score against Wimbledon every time I played at Plough Lane, and it became one of my favourite hunting grounds.

The following Monday I was retained in the side, and that was the kick-start for my first-team career. My next game was against Leicester, with Alan Smith playing for the opposition even though he had been signed by Arsenal. The deal was that, having made a commitment to join us, he should see out the sea-son for Leicester. With the North Bank chanting Alan Smith's name, we won 4-1.

It was not only a big start for my career; my drinking had also taken off. Whether that was my way of coping with my new-found fame and fortune I don't really know. It just came naturally to me. I was hitting the nightclubs with the big-name Arsenal stars. I thought I had arrived, rubbing shoulders with Charlie Nicholas and Graham Rix in the same top side in the country and the same top nightspots in London.

But I was about to get a very firm lesson in the ways of top-class football. It was at Manchester City and I was up against tough de-fender Mick McCarthy. The match kicked off, and when I went for the ball Mick McCarthy elbowed me straight in the face. He turned round instantly and said, 'Welcome to the big time, son!' Some welcome. I didn't touch the ball again and we lost 3-0. If he was trying to intimidate a raw eighteen-year-old, he certainly succeeded.

Yet I was determined to make my mark in football and at QPR we won 4-1. I got one of the goals and Graham Rix got a couple. It wasn't going to be an easy start, though. Soon I was up against the Nottingham Forest hard man the fans nicknamed 'Psycho' – the intimidating, tattooed Stuart Pearce, who would eventually become England captain. He had his own inimitable style of trying to sort me out. 'So you're the wise guy,' he said to me with that penetrating glare. It was a look that told me to stay clear of him. Yet not long after that first meeting on the pitch, he was the first to shake my hand when I was named as Young Footballer of the Year. He had probably voted for me. A few years later we were in the England squad together.

At this stage I didn't have a guaranteed place in the first team, but I found myself playing alongside some very experienced players in the reserves. Steve Williams, for one. To this day I believe he was the best midfield player that I have ever played with. Another player I greatly admired was the club's first-choice centre-forward, Paul Mariner, who played for England. He possessed exceptional skill for such a big man. Nial Quinn was even bigger. I played with Nial when he was sixteen and first came over from Ireland. We played together in the reserves at Southall and he scored four times – after coming on as a substitute.

I was an unselfish striker, always prepared to create goals as well as try to score them, but Steve Williams told me to 'go for goal'. This helped me to increase my goal output and got me noticed and back in the first team. Not everyone liked Steve. A tough nut who spoke his mind and was very clever, he had a real no-nonsense way with him. If anyone was slacking, he would 'hammer' him, shouting and screaming, even though it was only a reserve game with hardly a soul watching. But he tried to help me in various ways and gave me plenty of good advice. 'Look after yourself,' he told me, 'and you won't go far wrong.' I wish I had listened to him.

Instead I was easily swayed by the glamour of players of star status. I started going to places like Stringfellows and I suddenly developed an inflated ego and thought I was the dog's bollocks.

In 1985, the year after I got engaged to Lorraine, I called it all off. I told her I didn't want to settle down and wanted to enjoy myself going out with the lads and drinking. We had a row and went our own ways. Lorraine was broken-hearted. I was upset too, but I thought I knew what I was doing, and that I was doing the 'in' thing by hanging out with the boys. Having split with Lorraine, I had no stabilizing influence in my social life and I soon went off the rails once more. The more famous I became, and the more money I earned, the worse it got. Only now do I know what an idiot I've been and I hope that youngsters reading this will learn from my mistakes – and they were big mistakes.

Lorraine had kept in touch with mum and dad, and somehow it was inevitable that we would get back together. The on-off romance was back on after three months.

I went off on tour to Singapore, leaving it to Lorraine and my mum to go around the estate agents to find a house in Sandridge, near St Albans. I was happy with their choice, even though I hadn't seen it, and we moved in in 1985, paying a mortgage of £500 a month, with everything in the house on HP.

It wasn't really a good choice – the house was between two pubs! At that time, though, I thought it was a brilliant idea, as I was banned for a drink-driving offence and I could now walk to the pub. It was now becoming very difficult to get up in the morning. The drink-driving charge was the lowest point of my troubles so far. It was the worst thing that I had ever done, and I was rightly barred from Arsenal for two weeks. However, that suspension didn't bring me round, but only made me play up to my bad-boy image all the more. It was pathetic. I just loved to live up to my reputation. I was fined £350 for drink-driving and failing to stop at an accident and banned from driving for eighteen months.

It wasn't long before the rows Lorraine and I had been having got worse than ever. Angry scenes became almost routine, but neither of us thought much about it as they had become a way of life.

One Friday afternoon I came home from the betting shop after losing yet again. Lorraine was peeling potatoes when I walked in. We started to argue and I told her to fuck off and went upstairs to get changed out of my smoky clothes. All of a sudden Lorraine ran up the stairs with a knife in her hand. 'Put it down unless you're going to use it,' I said. I drove her into such a state of frenzy with my abuse that she pointed the knife at me and said she'd had enough of my gambling. 'You'll have to choose between me and gambling,' she went on. She just couldn't stand it any more. 'You'll have to go because I can't stop gambling. I love it more than anything and nothing will stop me,' I replied. She was so shocked that I chose gambling instead of her that she came towards me with the knife and drew it straight across the palm of my hand. She was very shocked when she realized what she had done and offered to take me to hospital immediately.

As we set off in the car she was very apologetic. But deep down I wasn't upset as I realized what I had said and just how much I'd hurt her by it. I ended up with ten stitches in my hand and Lorraine still felt sick at what she had done. But I knew how much I'd hurt her before and deep inside I knew that she was getting her revenge. Lorraine has never done anything like that again, as I think it hurt her very much. She is very calm, loving and caring and even after all the other problems I have put her through she has never again approached me the way she did that day.

Despite our up-and-down, highly volatile relationship, we still planned to marry. Hard to live together, impossible to live apart. We named the day for the wedding, but it wasn't long before we called it off. I didn't really feel that I wanted such a massive commitment as marriage. I wasn't ready for it; I was still very immature, still sorting my life out. One minute I wanted to marry Lorraine and settle down, the next I wanted to rush off with the superstars at the club and become a big shot off the field. I didn't knew at the time we broke off the wedding that Lorraine was pregnant with our first son, Charlie.

Drinking got me into deep trouble. Yet I still didn't understand the consequences. Quite the reverse, I considered myself to be Jack the Lad, a legend in my own mind! In front of the other players I felt 'big' and important because of my excesses.

I'd come home most nights around 4 a.m. from the local pub. Then I'd abuse Lorraine verbally, tell her to fuck off in front of everybody who'd come back with me. But the next day I wasn't the least bit ashamed of what I had done nor was I embarrassed in front of the same people who had witnessed my appalling behaviour. You would never hear me say I would not be seen in that pub again. The trouble was I would be completely paralytic yet again.

I didn't care how much I embarrassed Lorraine. We went to Ian Wright's barbecue with all the lads and their wives or girlfriends, and all the kids. Everyone was having a lovely time but when Lorraine said it was time to go home I just couldn't go. I had started drinking and I couldn't stop. I had to go on somewhere with a mate and didn't return home until five or six in the morning. The reality was that I couldn't leave anywhere, any place in the world, until I had exhausted all the drink. There were times when I would psych myself up before I'd take Lorraine out by telling myself, 'No matter what happens I'll be taking Lorraine home.' But I could never do it.

And yet the drink and the gambling never hindered my career. I was called up for the England under-nineteen side when Bobby Robson was manager and Don Howe was the coach. Michael Thomas and Neil Ruddock were in the side that went on a tour of South America. I spent most of my time in Brazil and Uruguay ringing Lorraine. I hated being away on tour and couldn't wait to get home. Being in exotic places like Rio de Janeiro meant very little to me. Even though my relationship with

Lorraine was on and off, I always missed her when I was away. It was that sort of thing that finally made me realize that I couldn't live without her and made me change my mind about making a commitment to her.

4

...AND YOU LOSE SOME

When I made the grade and got into the England under-twenty-one team in 1990, I was just one step from my first full cap at senior level. My first game was at Watford, playing up front with David Hirst, and we drew 0-0 with Denmark. My entire family turned out for that game. They must have nearly filled the stand!

I had to wait until I was twenty-three to make it into the England team. My debut was against the mighty Germans at Wembley. Coming on as a substitute for just the last thirteen minutes or so, I played up front alongside Gary Lineker. I nearly marked my first England appearance with a goal. I should have scored, and if I'd had a left foot I would have done!

My career was soaring. We had won the European championship in 1989, when I was twenty-one, and now again in 1991. The first championship had been achieved at Liverpool, and we went to Anfield needing to win by two goals. It was a formidable task, quite beyond most teams, and everyone expected it to be beyond us. Few experts, if any, gave us a hope in hell of doing it. We travelled up early that day and relaxed in a hotel before the evening's momentous match. Everyone was so laid-back about our assignment that it seemed unreal. My dad rang me at the hotel and I told him that everyone was looking forward to the task in a very relaxed mood.

The 'boss' gave his pep talk – keep it tight, keep the score to 0-0 at half-time, grab an early goal at the start of the second half and then get the winner at the end. Would you believe it? It went precisely to plan.

36

I was substituted in the last few minutes, at the same time as Steve Bould. My best mate, Perry Groves, took my place. It's not really the same when you are sitting on the bench and something as significant as a title win takes place. You really want to be on the pitch at the end. I suppose that is simply a professional's point of view. It happened to me again in the European Cup Winners' Cup Final in 1994 against Parma. I was taken off with just five minutes to go. Again it was a great night of celebrations. But for me it didn't diminish the magnitude of our success then and the previous season.

Returning to the season we won the European title in 1989, this must rank as my best of all time. I won the coveted Young Player of Year award, nominated by my fellow professionals as the outstanding young player of the season.

Yet behind the scenes my life was in total turmoil. Betting and boozing had taken a grip on my life. At the dinner and dance at the Grosvenor House Hotel to celebrate our championship win, I ended up drunk at the bar, completely missing the dinner. Instead of going to eat, I kept on drinking with one or two of the lads, but by the end of our sessions I had little or no idea who was drinking with me. We were creating so much noise that, even with the doors shut, the dinner guests couldn't hear the speakers, and the comedian was completely drowned out. The comedian that night was Norman Collier and although he didn't complain almost everybody else did! Worse was to come. There was a big fight outside the hotel and of course I was in the middle of it. I was paralytic, and I was in big trouble again.

The club had already given me three previous warnings about my behaviour, and they were furious this time. I was kicked out for two weeks. I was so upset, so crestfallen, that I had to hide myself away. I couldn't even go home because of the press, so I went to Lynn and John, my uncle and aunt in Kingsbury, to get myself together. The club had told me not to bother to come back unless I sorted myself out. I didn't show my face outside the club door, I felt so ashamed of myself.

I went back after the fortnight's suspension and promised faithfully that I was a reformed character. I made my return, coming on as a sub, against Manchester United in a 'live' TV match. The fans knew I had been disciplined by the club, and the incident, although not all the gory details, had been reported in the press. They were great to me, as usual. However, that wasn't really going to do me much good – it just encouraged me to play up my wild image.

We failed to retain the championship. It is not surprising really, because you are there to be knocked down and everyone wants to beat the champions. The season became a struggle to live up to our reputations.

But the following year we were so red-hot I really thought we'd go right through the season without losing a single game in the league. We lost only once, and that was at Chelsea when I felt that if Steve Bould hadn't left the field injured we would have lost at the Bridge. Without Bouldy at the back, Michael Thomas dropped back as an emergency centre-back.

Perhaps our thrashing by Manchester United at home in the Littlewoods Cup, a resounding 6-2 defeat, concentrated our minds and efforts on the championship. But I always felt we had a terrific side. Kevin Richardson might have been a moaner, but he was a great lad and a terrific leader. 'Angry Eyes', I called him. Brian Marwood's corners were as valuable as a penalty with Bouldy flicking the ball on at the near post and 'Rodders' (captain Tony Adams) steaming in at a hundred miles an hour. We were a team with massive belief in ourselves and plenty of ability.

However, all the glory, the big bonuses and the success made no difference to me. Except in one respect – the more I got, the more I spent. It wasn't long before I was up to my old tricks, only from then on I tended to make sure it wasn't under the nose of the club.

If my drinking was a problem, it was nothing compared to my gambling.

The day we moved into our second house, we were sitting there without a penny to buy a slice of bread. The house had cost us £136,000 at that time, just before we got married. By the time we moved in I had squandered every single penny on gambling. We had to go round to my mum and dad's for something to eat!

I even had a bet on my wedding day. The big day was 16 June 1990. It was also the middle of the World Cup finals in Italy. The ceremony took place at St Leonards Church, in Sandridge, close to our new home, but this was like any other day for me – betting and boozing.

In fact I'd had quite a bit to drink before we got to the church. 'Did I really do that?' I now say to myself. I found a nice little pub near the church and went in before tying the knot, to down about five or six double vodka and oranges. (I was advised not to indulge in my usual drink of lager because I'd be rushing off to the toilet all day, and that wouldn't go down too well, particularly during the wedding ceremony.) Because of the amount I was drinking by then, the vodka didn't have that much effect, and I was nowhere near drunk. I did it merely to calm my nerves.

More important for me was placing a bet. I used to like to place a bet in the morning and that would settle me down for the rest of the day, as if I had something in my life that was worth waiting for. I knew I could watch the World Cup games before the disco that night with a few of the Arsenal lads who were coming to the wedding. I didn't go for the England versus Holland match because it was hard to pick a winner from that one in a tight opening qualifying group, and as it turned out I was right, because it ended in a draw. There were 120 guests on my wedding day, but Lorraine's and my big day had begun with me handing my brother and best man £700 in cash to nip round the betting shop, before we all went to the church, to put it on Scotland – at 4-7 on, if I remember rightly – to beat Costa Rica.

So, on our wedding night I was glued to the TV. I sat riveted on the end of the bed on the first night of our honeymoon, watching my £700 disappear as Costa Rica beat Scotland 2-1. That's a compulsive gambler for you. A compulsive gambler can never win.

I spent an awful lot of time glued to the TV watching various of my bets coming to a sad end. I was once watching TV upstairs when I had placed a lot of money on a horse. At that time it would have been about £400 or £500, but it wasn't long before I was betting thousands. The horse was beaten on the line and I was so furious that I slung the TV set down the stairs, completely wrecking it. Lorraine, who was downstairs at the time, was shocked. But that's how it was beginning to affect me even in the early days.

Lorraine gave birth to our first son, Charlie, in December 1990. On the fourteenth the doctor told her that she had to go to hospital to be induced, and two days later, on the Sunday, she began having bad labour pains. Because it was our first, I wasn't really aware of what to expect. I began to panic. It was a lot to cope with at the age of twenty-two, and my way of dealing with it was to have a bet. I suggested that the best thing was for Lorraine to go to hospital. She drove herself there and I told her, 'If anything happens, give me a ring.' She was back home two hours later, finding me settled down watching the American football on television after placing a bet.

On Monday 17 December I arrived at the hospital for the birth, and they put me in a little room. From there I rang the bank manager to arrange a loan so that I could use the money for gambling. I spent the day at the betting shop and arrived back at the hospital at 5 p.m. I sent my mate out for a pizza and watched telly while Lorraine was in labour and giving birth. Her waters broke at 7 p.m., but by 2 o'clock in the morning I was fed up and asked the nurse, 'How long is it going to be now? There's nothing left to watch on TV.' Charlie was born at 5 a.m. and Lorraine returned home two days later.

For two days I had forgotten to buy Lorraine flowers. As I couldn't drive, because I was banned at the time, Lorraine's mum drove me to the nearest florist's and I grabbed the first bunch I could get my hands on. But on the way back from the shop I stopped off at the betting shop while she was sitting in the car waiting for me. There I was, flowers in hand, placing a bet.

The night before Charlie's christening, we went out for a meal.

I was drinking so much by this stage that I couldn't go home until I had polished off a bottle of brandy with a friend. Luckily his girlfriend was driving. On my way home in the car I was swigging back the brandy until I'd finished the entire bottle. But I managed to make it to the christening. Another time, after a friend's child's christening in Nottingham, I wouldn't go home until somebody gave me a six pack to drink on the way. Then there was a bar mitzvah where I was so paralytic that I was giving out my home telephone number and address. Out of the blue I got a call from a fourteen-year-old girl I had promised could come and stay with us! There were times when I'd go out and drink with people who'd ring me up and I'd never heard of them. It wasn't unusual for me to find a dozen business cards in my pocket from people who had been buying me drinks the night before.

I would get up to all sorts of dirty tricks to have a bet. When he was a little older I would leave Charlie in the car with the window wound down slightly, to run off to place a bet. I'd give him a fist full of betting slips to play with while I was in the bookie's.

I was at the hospital when Ben was born, on 15 April 1992. While Lorraine was being stitched up, I wheeled in the phone trolley on the pretence of ringing relatives, so I could make arrangements with some mates to meet up for a drink. I then went in to see Lorraine. She was starving and asked me to get her something to eat. I popped round to the nearest vending machine and came back with a corned beef sandwich. I'm sure she thought I was going to bring her back something much more substantial and interesting, like a pizza.

At Ben's christening I drank all day and insisted on having the TV wheeled in with all the guests still there so I could watch the Coca-Cola Cup Final with a few mates. The real reason I had to watch that game was that I had a bet on the outcome. That night I invited as many people as I could back to the house for another drinking session. It was midnight before everyone had gone.

Sometimes the first-team lads would have a night out at the dogs at Walthamstow. We'd finish our morning's training at Highbury at about 12.30 and then go to the pub for a few drinks.

By three o'clock I'd be off to place a bet or two. By five I might have lost the £500 I had on me, and by the time we decided to set off for the stadium I wouldn't have a penny left. One time I had to borrow £100 from one of my mates for my dinner at the dogs.

Did Lorraine object? Well, actually she didn't. She had become used to it. She thought this was the normal sort of life a footballer lives. And betting is a big problem in football – much bigger, perhaps, than many people realize – as it is in society as a whole. For me, betting was my enjoyment, and eventually took me over and became my life.

And then there was the drinking. Betting and drinking were a volatile cocktail for me. At its height, my drinking got so bad that I felt I was going crazy. Of course there was a gradual build-up, and at first it might have sounded like boyish pranks, but it grew into something evil.

After all the shit Lorraine had to put up with from me, it was pretty hard for her to take the verbal abuse I gave her when I had been drinking. I would throw her out of the house, and then shout at her as she was driving off because I couldn't understand why she was going. I'd throw stones at the car to stop her. We would have such terrible rows that I would kick her out, lock the door and go to bed, leaving her outside for an hour or so.

The poor people in my favourite Chinese restaurant would have to stay up with me in the small hours until I had drunk a bottle of Sambucca dry. Now they cannot believe the change in me – a diet Coke, a meal and straight home with Lorraine.

In the early part of the decade I was apparently still making an impact on the field. My touch might have been unimpaired, but my fitness was always a problem. I was playing on my reputation. George Graham knew I was grossly overweight at times, usually when I reported back from pre-season training. I'd pull off my shirt and breathe in to keep my stomach in. A number of times the boss spotted it and fined me for being overweight.

There were times when he gave me a 'last' warning and told me to get myself back into shape or else. I could still go a week without a drink, although it was getting harder each time. But there was no way I could go longer than that. There were times when I went without a drink for a few days, or as long as I could, to show some sort of improvement in my physical condition.

But it was getting tougher to go a day without drinking. If I was on antibiotics for a sore throat, I would have to stop taking them on a Saturday, even if I was nowhere near cured, so I could have a drink with the lads after a game.

When I was in good shape and in top form, there was a full England cap as my reward. I scored in a very tough away game against Czechoslovakia in 1992, playing up front with Mark Hateley, a big, bustling centre-forward I admire greatly. Mark is very experienced, having played with Glen Hoddle in Monaco after a spell in Italy with AC Milan. He was a big help to me in that game. I seem to recall that Martin Keown got a goal too. He was at Everton at that time, but has now rejoined us at Arsenal. Mark Hateley moved on to Glasgow Rangers, and in fact there was quite a bit of speculation at that time that the Scottish giants were keen on me.

My performance against the Czechs must have been good enough to launch me into the England European Championship squad, because in my next match, against Hungary, I had a nightmare of a game and was brought off at half-time. The way I got hammered in the media the next day, I thought that was the end of it and that I had no chance of ever playing for my country again. I would believe everything I'd read in the papers – to such an extent that I'd look up the ratings and if I'd got only a five out of ten I'd sulk for the rest of the week, but if I'd got a high rating I'd feel I was bound to be picked again. Even if the manager might think otherwise!

My reputation was well known throughout the game. I wanted to be one of the best, but I soon discovered what the people who really mattered thought about me. I was on the England tour of the USA, a year before the World Cup finals in 1994. Graham Taylor was the England manager and I had spent two weeks in the States without kicking a ball. Finally Taylor decided to play myself and John Barnes up front against Germany in our final match in Detroit's indoor Silverdome. We were doing some 'shadow play' in training and the players, including me, heard Taylor remark, 'Merson, now he's a good player. Only trouble is you don't know what will happen next, whether he'll be carried out of a taxi legless. Put a pint of lager in the middle of the goal and he'll get it.'

Ian Wright heard it, and so did John Barnes. Wrighty never fails to remind me of it. To be honest, when I heard him say it I thought to myself, yeah, he's right, that's me.

Funnily enough, the match against Germany was the best I've ever played for my country. But it had nothing to do with Taylor's jibe – I was just pleased to get a game after such a long wait.

It didn't really surprise me to learn what people thought of me. Why should it? In May 1990, together with three colleagues, I was sent home in disgrace from our club tour of Singapore. I was caught drinking the night before the last game of the season, away to Norwich, but I thought nothing of it because I was injured and wasn't even playing, although I knew it broke club rules. Nothing was said.

I was caught throwing a glass ashtray at someone in a night-club, and that's what I thought I was sent home for. But, as well as sending me home, the club also fined me the maximum two weeks' wages for drinking on a Friday night before a game. Instead of me thinking, That's it now, I've got to reform, it didn't really bother me. In fact I wanted to be known as the trouble-maker; I enjoyed it. Those were my wild days, and at the time I was proud of them.

While some of my exploits happened in private, there were a couple of things that were captured on camera and will for ever be images that people link to me. It will take a long time to persuade them to look at me in a different light, but I'm hoping this book will go a long way to achieving that. I want people to understand what has been happening to me.

The fans loved my wild-man image. I used to dream that I would run out at Highbury with the fans singing 'Wild Thing', just as they did to a baseball player in a film. I had been captured on TV signalling to friends in the crowd at Wembley by tipping my hand in a drinking motion. The fans called it 'Doing a Merson'. I did it first after Arsenal beat Spurs in the semi-final of the FA Cup in 1993, and again after our Cup Final replay victory over Sheffield Wednesday.

Now I'm haunted by that image, and cringe whenever I see it. But that was then and this is now. I've got to start building my life and reputation again. It's not going to be that easy convincing people that I am a reformed character. I keep on hearing the whisper that I have returned to my old ways. No chance.

But it is betting that has been my real downfall, and I have no intention of going back to my old ways. They used to say about Stan Bowles that if he could pass a betting shop the way he passes a ball he would have been a regular in the England team. Well, I am determined to pass every betting shop and get back into the England team.

5

GAMBLING WITH EVERYTHING

In all, I must have gone through around £2000 worth of co-caine. That was just what I spent out of my own pocket. There must have been much more coke that I was given by people that I didn't pay for. It had started off as an experiment, but it got to the stage where I just had to have the stuff. It almost ruined my life. I had jeopardized my career and my marriage. I wanted everyone to know what had happened, because then I could put it all behind me and start with a clean slate. I wanted to stop all the worrying – so much worry that it was driving me insane, pushing me to breaking point.

It was my first serious venture into drugs. I started taking cocaine – known on the streets as 'Charlie' – in January 1994 be-cause my footballing career had hit such a low point. I was deeply depressed because of my huge, stupid gambling debts. I was con-vinced that I could never become an addict. Now I know that I was in real danger of much worse than taking cocaine. When I went out I just had to have the drug. It made me feel so much more confident. And a bonus was that I could drink all night without feeling sick.

I took my first line of cocaine in a Hertfordshire pub toilet. It seems so tacky now when I look back at my antics, so awful, and I don't really know how I came to sink so low. Then again I do. I was feeling about as low as I could get and had gone to the pub with a group of friends and Arsenal supporters. I was asked by a pal, 'Do you want a bit of Charlie?' I'd had about eight or nine pints of lager top – all I would normally take – and until then the only time I had ever experimented with drugs was when I was about sixteen and smoked some dope. But at that time just about everyone I know had. When I was at school nobody had really even heard of cocaine, and that was only eleven years ago.

I was anxious about taking coke and worried about what the effects would be – perhaps I'd go off my head. I thought it might be like LSD and I would start having hallucinations. I wouldn't have even thought about it if I hadn't been drunk. But I decided to give it a try. We all went into the toilet, and it didn't even occur to me there might be other people around thinking it was odd – three blokes in the same cubicle. One of the guys opened a piece of paper holding the coke, emptied it on top of the toilet cistern and cut it into two three-inch lines for me to take. The other one rolled up a £5 note, and I just sniffed the stuff up my nose.

At first it didn't seem to give me a buzz at all and it was a bit of an anti-climax. But when I went back into the bar I suddenly found myself chatting to everybody, including girls, and I felt super-confident. Normally I'm quite shy, especially if I'm sober, and I wouldn't want to talk to anybody I didn't know. But that night I started rabbiting on to all sorts of people. I felt I could talk to anybody. The only other effect that I noticed was that I had started grinding my teeth. Otherwise, I felt great. It's not that harmful after all, I thought. I went back to the toilets twice more and started to really like it.

Around midnight I headed home by taxi to Lorraine, who at the time was six months pregnant, and Charlie, who was three, and Ben, who was just eighteen months. The strange thing was, even though I'd had so much to drink I felt wide awake. Normally I need eight hours' sleep, but that night I had only three and was as bright as anything the next morning. Lorraine didn't suspect anything because I was in the guest bedroom, where I usually went after I'd been out drinking. At the time, I just thought it was one of those things I would never try again. My attitude was, well, everyone tries it once. I put it down to experience. But I did notice that day that I was very lively around the house, and I didn't have any trace of a hangover. Usually I would have had a blinding headache. The risk of being exposed didn't even occur to me because I trusted the people I was with.

In the coming months I never risked buying directly from a dealer and I certainly never took cocaine to enhance my performance during a game. The thought never crossed my mind, because I knew, if anything, it would only have a harmful effect, although when I was taking it, that thought never came into my mind either.

This is great, I said to myself after that first experiment. I can go out drinking all night and be as right as rain the next day. It was true that I was depressed at the time. But to say that it led to my attachment to the drug is a feeble excuse. In fact a bit of success on the field – after the low of being left out of the team – encouraged me to have another session within a few weeks.

On Saturday, 19 February I played against Everton at Goodison Park. It's a date and a game I will never forget. As I was picking up the ball in the opposition half, I spotted Neville Southall off his line and scored with a chip that I would rank as one of my best. Not bad as Neville is an experienced and brilliant Welsh international keeper. I was on a real high, and got a pat on the back from the boss. I wanted to celebrate. As soon as I got off the coach I went straight to the same Hertfordshire pub as before. That was the night I tried cocaine for the second time. Like before, I'd drunk quite a few lager tops, but this time I knew the score. I was definitely interested in trying the drug again. My mate said he had some and I think I paid him about £50 for it. I took it by the same method – going to the toilet and cutting it with a credit card. I must have gone in there four or five times that evening.

I never really got into all the special words they used. And I had no idea of the quantities I was taking or what it was worth. It had the same effect on me again. I was chatting to everybody, feeling confident and not at all tired. We all went on to a country club a few miles away. I was there for two or three hours and then got a cab home. I couldn't sleep until about 5 a.m. and was awake – zing! – at 8 o'clock, as lively as anything. I felt all stuffed up and when I blew my nose into a tissue I noticed there was some blood on it. That worried me a bit, and I wondered how it had got there. I also noticed that my nose was itching all the time.

As the season drew to a close, and I prepared for a much-needed family holiday, I didn't try cocaine again for a number of weeks. But on returning from the holiday I was ready for more. As soon as I got home I told Lorraine that I was just popping round to my friend's house to drop off some presents we'd bought on holiday, and would only be about ten minutes. When I got there, my mate said he had some gear on him and we got stuck into it. We must have done about seven lines each. Oddly, even though we were in his house, we still went into the toilet to do it. The effect was the same as usual. It keeps you awake and makes you want to talk more. We just chatted and chatted and I didn't leave until about 2 a.m. It was lucky that Lorraine had already gone to bed so that it didn't occur to her that something was wrong.

I knew that using cocaine would shock Lorraine if she ever found out because she had absolutely no idea what was going on. I was determined that she wouldn't find out because I was frightened what she would do. In short, I was scared she would walk out on me. She had threatened to do that as I was behaving so badly, but I never really believed she would. I knew I was being an idiot. I knew I was risking everything that was so precious to me, but I couldn't help myself. After all I'd done it would have been no surprise if she had packed her bags and left me. It would have been no more than I deserved.

As well as keeping my habit a secret from Lorraine, I never told even my team-mates. I never shared the drug with any of them, despite all the malicious rumours that I did. But I first really began to worry about being detected within the game when our club doctor, John Crane, gave the team a lecture on the drug problem in football. The doc warned the players there was such a problem – it had to be crushed and there were plans for random drug testing. He also talked of the effects of too much drinking.

All the lads were larking about and joking, not taking it seriously. But I was dead silent and worried about what the doc was saying. When he mentioned drug tests I was terrified and thought I wouldn't have a chance. I thought there must have been rumours going around that I was on drugs and that they had reached the club. To my great relief, nothing came of it.

But it scared me half to death, so I decided to lay off the stuff. But then another injury led me back to it. It was at the end of September. I had injured an ankle during training and I was out of the team again and depressed. To relieve the boredom I began gambling heavily again.

I was losing all the time and it all got on top of me. I just started going out more often, drinking and taking drugs. I'd go out at least once a week and have up to fourteen pints of lager top. I never drank anything else. I was also doing line after line of cocaine throughout the night. It was the only way I felt I could cope with all the debts. I'd just walk out the door, go to a nightclub in West London and get completely out of my head. But one of the most depressing things about it all was that I started to forget my family life. And I've always been a big family man. I began to hate myself. Yet there seemed nothing I could do about it, as I never knew that I needed specialist treatment to save me from myself.

I knew just how close I had come to being exposed as a drug-taker, as I had heard all the rumours, and I had become aware of ugly insinuations, exaggerations of my 'crimes'. I was deeply concerned about the consequences of being found out. The amount of stories I started to hear about myself were just incredible, and certainly not true. I'd been in the manager's office at times and he'd pointed at me and said, 'You've been out with so and so last night,' when in fact I'd been at home with Lorraine. It was happening so much that I'd become paranoid – so paranoid so that I was beginning to wonder whether I was really there or not. When you keep on hearing the same rumour, even though you know it didn't happen to you, your mind plays tricks and you begin to wonder. I wanted to get the whole truth out in the open because

I was convinced it was the only way that would ultimately help me. I couldn't have gone on any longer without talking about it fully, and I just hope people will say that at least the guy was big enough to open up about his problems.

I really thought I had been rumbled by the press when I found reporters waiting for me outside my home. After breaking my nose in a game against Leeds in August, I was booked into St Mary's Hospital, Paddington, to have it reset. I was contacted by George Graham, who said a journalist had phoned to claim I'd checked out of a drug clinic in West London. He and I knew that it was ridiculous and that I'd been in hospital to have my nose re-set. At the back of my mind I was worried somebody might have said something. That night I got home and reporters from a national newspaper were outside my house and they repeated the allegation that I'd checked out of a drugs clinic. I just said it was a load of nonsense and that I'd been in St Mary's. They seemed to accept it and left it at that. Who's trying to grass me up? I was thinking. Someone must know that I'd been taking drugs.

This was the kind of thing you got from papers, I said to Lorraine, and told her to forget about it. But I vowed there and then I'd never take the drug again.

At the same time gambling got as tight a hold on my life as it had done for many years. It never became a massive problem until nearly two years ago, in 1993, when it just got completely out of control and I was placing bets of £5000, sometimes even £10,000, in one day on horse-races and anything else I could bet on – even things I knew absolutely nothing about, like bowls, darts, rugby and even the Eurovision Song Contest! I had an account with several firms and I could place bets with no questions asked. It got to the stage where I was so bored and depressed after I injured my ankle at the end of September 1994 that I just had to have a bet to get through the day. I would stop every morning at the newsagent's to pick up the *Racing Post* and I would scour through it until training began.

As soon as I'd finished training I'd go straight to the canteen and study the form of horses until I'd decided on a bet and then I would go off and phone in my bets. Losing didn't bother me too much and the betting firms aren't going to say no to the money. Every Sunday I would bet on the results of American football games and I would just sit in front of the TV and watch the results flashing up on Teletext from six p.m. until about midnight. I was such a compulsive gambler that as soon as I had a bet on I felt relaxed. I was satisfying the craving by placing the bet and I just kept putting more and more on. It was just greed, but I didn't have a single win for three weeks on the trot, and got more and more in debt. It became completely ridiculous.

At one stage I was even tuning in to listen to American football games on the American Forces Radio network, which broadcasts on medium wave in Britain. I would put a big bet on even though I didn't know the players' names or whose side they were on. Lorraine knew that I was taking a keener than normal interest, but she thought I was only placing small bets – say, £50 or £100.

Most of these bets were double or treble accumulators based on winning scorelines. I lost £10,000 betting on the Miami Dolphins against the Minnesota Vikings, and blew £20,000 on the Arizona Cardinals versus the Dallas Cowboys. I put a total of £5000 on eight other games. They were straightforward bets on the winner of a game, and the odds were virtually even or around 10-11. But I didn't have a single win. The fact that I was losing so much money never stopped me. It just made me put more and more on.

Lorraine might have known how often I was betting, but she didn't realize how much I was losing. She once said she would leave me if I didn't stop betting, but she didn't have a clue about the disease. Naturally I kept these huge debts a secret from her. But matters came to a head on 10 November, when I went out on one of my regular drinking sessions. A friend called to inform me that Lorraine had been tipped off about my gambling. The friend also told me she had spoken to George Graham. By then rumours about my excesses had reached Lorraine, and it was only natural that she should be worried sick. She was so worried to the point of not knowing where to turn and she ended up discussing my problems with my manager. But of course no one knew the true extent of those problems – not even me.

When I returned home I was confronted by Lorraine, who told me what she had done. It was so hard to take that I went out on a real bender. I knew I should have gone home and sorted it all out there and then, but I just went off my head, completely crazy. I was already getting drunk and one of my friends had some gear and I just started taking line after line after line of it. There was no way I was going to go back and I could never say no to a drink once I'd started.

I stayed out that night and just got totally out of my head. I didn't get in from a nightclub until about six in the morning. When I eventually got home I just lay on a bed in the spare bedroom and cried my eyes out – I thought the world had fallen in on me. I cried myself to sleep and when I woke up in the morning Lorraine was going spare and I told myself, this has got to stop now for all our sakes.

All I know is that I decided to finish with the drug there and then. I couldn't go on living a lie. My home life was hell, especially for Lorraine because I was becoming a monster, and I don't know to this day how she put up with me.

When I got home that night I said to myself, 'You're behaving like a twenty-one-year-old rather than a father with two kids and another on the way.' I just said to myself that it had to stop and it did, although not at first, and certainly it wouldn't have done if I hadn't had treatment.

My one-night stand took place on that night, 10 November. I was at my lowest ebb. Lorraine was six months pregnant and had just been told that I had run up massive gambling debts. I felt completely unable to cope with the strain and I thought my soccer career might be over. Tormented with worry, I went on a five-hour binge with pals. I took line after line of cocaine after downing pints of lager top. We went to the Boulevard night club in Ealing. Normally I'm so shy that I wouldn't chat to girls. But I was so high on cocaine that I was chatting to this bird all night.

I must have looked a right state but I don't think it bothered her. Later I went back to her house. I can't even remember where we made love, I was so out of my head. I can't remember the girl's name. That's God's honest truth. She was a nice girl, but I can't believe now that I made love to her. I feel terrible about it and how it might affect what people think of me. At the time it happened, I was in total despair. I didn't know what to do.

I had taken a taxi from the Boulevard to the girl's house, and another from there back home. If Lorraine had asked why I had stayed out so late I would have said that I had been to another late-night club in Dover Street, in the West End, which stayed open later than the Boulevard.

After January I started taking a lot of cocaine and found it a lot easier to start talking to birds. It never went farther than that, except for that one occasion. I've heard all sort of wild stories about me, including one in which I was supposed to have been caught half-naked with a bird in the executive box at Highbury. That is complete and utter nonsense. But so many people have asked me about it, and I've been in such a state, that I've even wondered at times whether it could be true. No, it definitely isn't. I just wish I could turn the clock back and start all over again. I've done some terrible things of which I'm truly ashamed.

The next morning Lorraine demanded to know exactly all the trouble I was in, as she had reached the end of her tether. She was now saying she would leave me. I admitted to the gambling disasters, but couldn't bring himself to admit to cheating on her and to taking cocaine.

I knew precisely the moment my football career had reached the point of disaster. It was 3 November 1994 in Arsenal's Cup Winners' Cup tie with Danish side Brondby at Highbury.

I had been living a monumental lie. It had been sheer hell and I desperately wanted people to know, as deep down I knew I needed some sort of help. It had affected my performances and I realized that in the Brondby game. It just hit me. I was drained, everything got on top of me. I couldn't run. It was the worry, the sheer stress, the anguish I was causing to myself. The mere act of moving was painful, everything seemed to be an utter effort. I couldn't concentrate on the game, and by the end I was just praying we would get through.

It was the sheer mental torture of keeping this sad secret to myself that bled me dry of energy – not the effects of drugs. It all finally hit me, it all caught up with me – at the age of twenty-six I could end up having thrown everything away. It was frightening and I knew a lot of people were going to be very surprised at what had happened to me.

I never took cocaine before a match. I only took it when I wasn't playing, and that's why there was never any chance of anything being found in my system if I had ever been given a drugs test. But finally I knew that bingeing on booze and cocaine had seriously affected my physical condition. Even so, they actually had one positive side-effect. The sheer worry, all the stress – bottling all this up for so long had caused me to lose a stone in weight. I was back to my best weight of 12st 12lb, after ballooning to a disgusting, embarrassing weight of 13st 10lb. Bouldy is four or five inches taller than me and powerfully built, but he only weighed 2lb more than I did. I'd been so worried sick those past few weeks that my guts had been turning over. I'd been shaking, a bag of nerves. When all my problems began to affect me really badly, my weight was up, my fitness was down. I couldn't even be bothered to get out of bed in the morning to train. Lazy! There wasn't anyone lazier than me. I didn't want to train – I just wanted to let everything go.

George Graham knew most of it – not everything, certainly not at the time – but I had to tell him as much as I could. I worried that when it all came out the boss would have second thoughts about giving me another chance and perhaps nobody else would want to buy me either. But I still thought that I was good enough provided I got myself right.

And I was always defiant, even through my darkest moments. For God's sake, I told myself, I was only twenty-six; surely I had time on my side. I should have five years left at the top. I was in Terry Venables's first two England squads, I played against Greece and I personally thought that on my day I was still good enough to play for England. Of course, by the time I had cracked up on the field I was far from being on my day! My aim was to get back to playing to the sort of form that first got me into the Arsenal and then England team under Graham Taylor and I was determined to give it my best shot. My mind had been on everything but football. But I knew I had to get my mind straight and get on with my life and with playing football again. The club had stuck by me and I owed them. I owed them and the fans in a big way and I planned to pay them back in a big way – and that was to turn up as the real Paul Merson.

I had to rely on George Graham and my team-mates if I was to succeed. None of the players knew at first, because I knew how much they would be shocked and they were. I knew that when they read my confessions it would knock them back. But I've got some very good friends at the club and I was sure they'd stand by me. In fact, I expected them to. That's the sort of team-mates they are. We have all stuck together in the past. I knew they would be surprised by this – shocked, in fact.

Gambling was the vice that crippled me financially and caused so many of the problems with Lorraine. Gambling was the first addictive thing that took a grip of my life, and that had a knock-on effect, as my relentless gambling increased my desire to drink heavily, and both excesses pushed me toward drugs.

I had plenty of critics queuing up to knock me after I confessed to my problems. They failed to understand that the public confession was part of my treatment. I had to get it all out in the open.

But the stories that were made up about me were so hurtful. It has been suggested that I ran up debts of £400,000. Utter rubbish. The day I drove to Gamblers Anonymous for the first time I was in debt to betting firms, friends and associates. People lent me money, but I was determined to pay them back and I have done so. On the other hand, I did squander up to £20,000 in a weekend betting on televised American football during one particular outrageous six-week frenzy that also involved drinking and drug-taking. I was slowly going off my head.

Violence was always simmering under the surface, basically because I didn't have control of myself. Now I wonder how I could have behaved so badly, particularly with the kids around. When I got depressed over my constant gambling losses, I attacked Lorraine in a terrible fit of rage. I knew that that wasn't the real me, but I was powerless to control myself. My life was spinning out of control. I just suddenly went berserk. I started throwing things around the house and smashing the place up. I punched Lorraine on the arm, and went to grab her by the throat. But I managed to restrain myself from actually throttling her. It was all over nothing. I can't even remember what she said that set me off. But it was all because the gambling debts were getting on top of me. Lorraine couldn't believe it; nor could I believe that I'd actually hit her. She went white as a sheet and was speechless with shock. She phoned the police and two male officers in a panda car came round. They took me into the kitchen to talk to me. Lorraine was in the other room in tears. One of the officers said to me I know who you are, you've got to calm down or we'll have to take you to the station and make it official, then everyone will get to know about it.

I'm still amazed it didn't get into the papers – for about a year I worried that it would – and I'm grateful it didn't leak out in any other way. It wasn't the real Paul Merson that night. I bitterly regret what I did. It's a totally shameful thing to happen and I swear I'll never do it again. I'm not an aggressive person. Whatever anyone else might say about me, even when I'm drunk I never hit people. The only way I can explain it was that I was off my head with worry and was not acting in a normal way.

Often I would smash the house up, kick in the wardrobe doors, put my fist through the walls. In May 1994 I threw Lorraine down the stairs in one of my drunken rages. I didn't mean to do it. She slipped. But we were having an argument, as I always did when I drank too much. Poor Charlie saw it. Next day when Lorraine's cousin, Pauline, came round, Charlie said to her, 'Daddy threw mummy down the stairs.' Naturally she was alarmed. We had to explain to Charlie that it was an accident. It was a terrible time. But when it was happening, it was something I thought was funny.

On the field I was still getting by without anyone noticing a deterioration in my fitness levels. We won the European Cup Winners' Cup, beating holders and favourites Parma, but my international career was in decline after a nightmare game against Greece even though England won 5-0 in one of Terry Venables's early games as manager of the team. I played the entire game but I was terrible and I put it down to my problems. I never got picked again.

It was my insanity that led me down the road to cocaine. There were two Paul Mersons. The gambler, the drinker, the drug user out of his head. Then there was the Paul Merson who was devoted to his family and dedicated to football. That's the man I want to prove I can become again, and I believe I'm doing just that, as there is nowhere for me to go if I fail now.

The good side of me was a person who would chat to everybody, always wanted to be with his family, playing with his kids, signing autographs for all the fans. The bad side was the short-tempered person who didn't care, didn't want to get involved with anybody, and kept himself to himself. And that was not the real me. I wanted the real Paul Merson to come out and now I never want to see the dark side again because I know that would be the end of me. All I knew then was that I wanted to get all my problems off my chest and out into the open. I urgently needed help. I'm so glad I got it.

No matter how desperate I became I was always clear enough in my mind to try to ensure that dabbling with drugs and excessive drinking did not affect my football. I was careful not to take drugs before a game because I always suspected it would have a bad effect rather than enhance my playing. The same went for training. I never used the drug before training.

The truth is that it did affect my professional life, for the more

I indulged the lower my form dipped. I couldn't have carried on much longer. As it is, what I have done to myself may have cut short my career by years. But if I hadn't stopped I would not have lasted more than a few days, let alone a few more years!

There was nobody in the team I could really confide in, so I kept my drug problem to myself. I didn't know of any other players who took cocaine, but I am not surprised now that other players have been involved with drugs. There is no one out there really warning them of the dangers, apart from the new FA programme, and I'm one hundred per cent behind and involved with that.

I knew Lorraine was going to be devastated when it all came out in the open. I knew how much the truth would hurt her, but it was important that she knew the truth. And, just as important, I needed to confess, as I couldn't have kept those terrible secrets to myself a day longer. I wanted the world to know everything because I was anxious to make a new start. I was not seeking sympathy, but just wanted people to give me a chance to prove I could behave professionally and be a good father to my kids and a good husband to my wife.

I knew it was not going to be easy, but nothing had prepared me for just how hard it was going to be. All the same, I had to try. If I carried on taking cocaine I knew it would end in an even bigger disaster than I was already facing. Who knows where it could have led to? You hear of people starting off on cocaine and then moving on to heroin. Can you imagine what effect that would have had on me? The sad truth is I don't really have any mates. A lot of people only talk to me because of who I am. The same goes for girls I meet, and that makes you feel sick.

My big worry at that stage was that confessing to drug-taking would wreck my career. I had been given a week by George Graham to sort out my life and regain my fitness. I was so naive that I really thought I'd be back in the first team after that week! I never imagined what I would have to go through to find a solution to my addictive nature. I had been given club permission to take a week's leave to straighten out the mess, because George had always wanted to help me. When I went out of the country,

I trained in the gym every day under the delusion I would be welcomed back in the team after a week. But I felt good that the club were standing by me, as I had been told the doors of Highbury were still open to me – although I knew I wouldn't be given any more chances. This was definitely my last chance.

Not many people will believe it, but there are two sides to George Graham and I've seen the other side – a very understanding man. If anyone was going to save me as far as my football was concerned, it would be him. I had made up my mind that I would pay him back on the football field by returning to Highbury as the old Paul Merson, as I knew this had to be not just the last chance from him, but the last chance I was giving myself. If I failed to sort myself out this time, I knew I was finished.

Graham might have been a dragon to some of the biggest Arsenal stars of the past, but he had been a father figure to me, saving my career as many as four times. And now he stood by me again. Of course, at first I had no idea that he was hiding his own personal nightmare over the 'bung' allegations that were ultimately to cost him his job at Highbury. I didn't find out until he had worked on getting me back into the team, fully rehabilitated, fully fit and fully integrated into the side once more.

The gaffer can be hard, even ruthless and we've all seen that side of him at the club. But I've also seen a different side to the man. The lads will tell you that the boss has given me a hundred chances, but in reality it is true he has bailed me out three or four times. I had plenty of last chances, but this was really it. No one knew just how much he had helped me sort out my problems in the past. He had always stuck by me and that's despite the amount of trouble I'd caused him. I will be for ever grateful for his best piece of advice: 'Try and keep your wife, save your marriage – that's your priority.'

I knew there was a massive risk that the Football Association might not be as understanding as my club. I knew I was the first Premier League player to confess to a drug-taking habit and that that left me wide open to a lengthy ban. However, I was always convinced that I wouldn't be suspended. When I look back I know I was probably deluding myself, as I really didn't know the impact that it had had. I just knew that my case was vastly different to that of Diego Maradona, who had been suspended for fifteen months from world football for far more serious links with cocaine than me. He had another ban after being drug-tested positive at the World Cup. His Argentinian team-mate Cannigia had also been banned for drug taking, but again he had been tested positive after a match.

I have vowed to myself that I won't take any substances, won't place another bet and won't take a drink. I can't even buy a lottery ticket. For me, it's far more difficult than giving up cocaine. I wasn't hopelessly addicted to drugs but I am a gambling addict through and through and the fact that I have to face is that there is no cure and that I will be fighting the craving for the rest of my life. But there is hope.

The meetings I now go to at Gamblers Anonymous are absolutely vital. It was so important to me to hear other people talking who have exactly the same problems and who have been through what I have been through. I think I will always have a bet in me, but I know that I can't because I'd risk losing everything – my family, my career and my whole life. I hope that I have the strength to continue to avoid temptation and stay away from gambling, drink and drugs.

GA was the first of the groups that I went to with the help of my sponsor, Steve Jacobs. Lorraine now attends GamAnon for the wives, with her sponsor, Mandy, Steve's wife.

I'd known Steve for some time, and he has become a really good and close friend. Once we were in a restaurant with Nigel Winterburn some years ago. Steve told us that he went to GA and, of course, we were all inquisitive asking him, 'What do you do there?' I never thought for a minute that one day I'd be going there, because you never think you yourself will become addicted to gambling or anything else. So I didn't believe him when he turned round to me and said, 'You'll probably be there in a year's time.' I couldn't see it, but Steve could. He could see the steady progression towards addiction to gambling.

In November 1994, a week before I confessed to all my addictions, Steve took me to GA for the first time. It was an awesome experience. I was scared stiff. I was frightened because I didn't know what to expect there.

I had good reason to be fearful. On that first night I had to get up before everyone and talk to them about my problems. I was quite close to tears. I could hardly talk. There I faced the first unnerving experience of self-analysis before similarly affected people, and I really wanted to pour out my troubles to that group of twenty strangers. There can be anything between fifteen and thirty people in a group. But all I managed to tell everyone was that I had started betting out of sheer habit rather than anything else and I was struggling badly with gambling debts. That's all I got out, and that was hard enough.

But I have come to enjoy these meetings, not fear them. Everyone is treated the same. You address the group by your first name. It doesn't matter whether you drive to these meetings in a Rolls-Royce or go by bus. If you have lost all your money at the bookie's it doesn't matter how much you once had!

6

OPENING UP

My life was such torment that I actually felt like killing myself. I used to drive home in my car and seriously think, should I pull over in front of this lorry? It got that bad. I'd hit rock bottom and I just couldn't handle it any more.

I knew I had to do something, and I felt the only way out was to come clean about my problems and try to sort them out one way or another. At the same time as wanting to make a clean breast of it, my biggest fear was being found out. I'd become so paranoid that I would end up driving in any direction to try to avoid someone following me, even though there was no one on my trail. When there was a car behind me for more than a few minutes I would take a left or right, turn in anywhere, even if it took me out of my way. I would be convinced that there was a pressman following me.

One night my dad dropped me off at a local hotel to meet up with the team. But when we set off there was a car parked nearby and when I got into the hotel I was in a terrible state. I rang my dad to check that the car we had seen earlier was still there, and what the driver was doing, if there was one. Of course, it was all innocent, but it illustrates the sheer fear of detection and why it was becoming too much of a burden to keep all my dark secrets to myself. I couldn't cope, carrying such a burden of guilt. I urgently needed help.

My decision to confess was a cry for help. I was advised that the best thing to do was to go public. People might not like what I had to say, but I hoped they would feel that I was big enough to have admitted to my problem. I have no regrets about speaking out. I could no longer live a lie. I wanted the good Paul Merson to win over the bad. I wanted the Football Association to know I was determined to become a reformed character. I wanted to change my life around.

So, after training on Thursday 24 November, I went to the office of a friend, Jerome Anderson, to tell my story to *Daily Mirror* sports writer Harry Harris, whose paper had arranged for a news reporter, Bill Akass to cover the story as well. I sat on the sofa in the offices above an estate agency in Edgware feeling relieved that it was all coming out in the open at last. I knew it would be a massive weight off my shoulders.

I had already spoken to Harry by phone the day before while he was in Göteborg, Sweden, reporting on Manchester United's European Cup tie and that night I spent two hours with Bill in Jerome's compact office, in the presence of Jerome's partner, Jeff Weston.

It was around 2.10 on a bright Thursday afternoon when I arrived at the meeting after my training stint. It was a typical day for me at that time. I felt lethargic. I was unshaven, wearing a polo shirt, looking worn out and gasping for food. I settled for a sandwich and a can of Coke.

For the next five hours the atmosphere in that office was electric. What I detested most was the filthy, horrible lies and distortions that were being put around about me, in and outside the press. They made me feel even more depressed, and even more determined that I was doing the right thing to get the truth across.

Thousands of words were filed that evening to the copytakers at the *Daily Mirror* headquarters in Canary Wharf by Harry and Bill. Because of the paper's need for total secrecy, it was decided that my story would have a code-name. Harry suggested Frank Worthington.

Lorraine had no idea what was going on. She knew about my gambling debts, and thought I was doing another big story about that. I had given an interview before to the *News of the World*. But Lorraine was bemused as to why there was such a need to get out of the country so quickly. Finally, to settle her mind, she decided to speak to George Graham, who advised her to go. Lorraine had spoken with the Arsenal manager a couple of times in the past about me and my problems, and now again she turned to him for advice. Once advised by Graham that it was in everyone's interests that she should leave the country with me for a while, Lorraine at least felt she was doing the right thing, although she still wasn't quite sure why it was necessary.

We were anxious to be abroad when the papers came on sale the next morning. We knew that there would be a hullabaloo, but we didn't know how big it would be. First Lorraine and I were going to take the kids, then that seemed impractical. Florida, to give the wife and kids a holiday, and somehow a suitable setting to tell her the dreaded truth, was my first choice. But I could appreciate the need not to fly too far from London in order to keep in daily touch with the trio of *Mirror* journalists accompanying us and our red-hot story. As time passed it became less likely that we would find a direct scheduled flight to Florida, so it was suggested we go to Paris overnight and then on to the States. The alternative was to find a safe house on the south coast of England or near the airport and make the journey the next morning, but I wasn't happy about either plan. New York was put forward as another suggestion, but again there was no flight available that night.

Eventually we were able to make arrangements for my mum and dad to look after the kids. We planned to fly to Paris in the expectation of getting on a flight to New York the next day. When I rang my parents about the kids my dad asked me about tickets for Saturday's game with Manchester United, but I couldn't tell him anything that was going on.

With time running out to make our escape, Bill and I left Jerome and Harry in the office, where they were joined by Jerome's assistant Stuart. Bill and I met Lorraine at Heathrow. All the time I was worrying how I would tell her what was going on. What was worse, I feared that she would leave me.

It wasn't until the plane got off the ground that I told Lorraine the first part of my confession – that I'd been taking cocaine. As I opened up I was frightened that she would go straight back home as soon as we touched down and not want to see me again. When we landed in Paris she wasn't too disturbed by what I'd revealed, but I still had to tell her about the girl and I was shitting myself.

There was a touch of humour that night, but I didn't find out about it until days later when I was sitting back at home with Lorraine watching 'Have I Got News For You' on TV. The *Mirror*'s big rival, the *Sun*, had been tipped off around 11.30 p.m. about a big story about to break. They were told the *Mirror* was running a drugs exposé about Paul Merton! The story goes that the editor of the *Sun* dispatched his news hounds to Merton's Fulham home. His wife apparently didn't take too kindly about being bothered at that time of night. He might be a famed comedian, but Paul Merton didn't find anything funny about that mix-up ! Naturally it merited a wry mention on the TV show.

We arrived that night in Paris, and checked into the hotel under the name Mr and Mrs Smith. Not exactly original, but it proved effective enough. I was petrified of being discovered by other journalists. But I felt comfortable with Bill and the *Mirror* photographer Arnie Slater.

The next day the story was hotting up and we had to change hotels in an attempt to avoid the press. We spent a night in a hotel in the centre of the city, but finally it was thought best that we get away from the capital, so we flew to the South of France. We had abandoned all notion of New York when someone told us that the press in the States might latch on to the story – and that it was pretty cold at that time of year. We went to a lovely hotel in Cannes. I had begun to confess to Lorraine bit by bit, but I had to carefully choose the right time to tell her everything, and decided to wait until we were settled in.

My other big fear was the reaction of the Football Association. My simple message to them was, 'Don't kick me out of football.' In one of my interviews I had said, 'I haven't brought the game into disrepute – I've brought myself into disrepute. I hope the FA don't ban me.' Even at this stage I was full of deep regret and I wanted to do something about it. I don't think I hurt the game of football. That was certainly never my intention and something I would never wish to do. I'd hurt myself and my family more than I'd hurt the FA. I'd been big enough to come forward and tell everyone what was happening to me. I could only hope that I would be able to stop it all and reform. I also hoped the FA would take that into consideration. The main point I wanted to make in my defence was that I was not doing it to enhance my performance. That was the last thing on my mind; it was never my intention.

The FA suspected drug-taking went on but had no idea of the extent of the number of players involved, and nor did I. Clearly they were concerned, because they started random checks at training grounds, targeting teenage professionals.

The criticism I was receiving hurt me. But not everyone slagged me off. I was grateful to George Best, who praised me on television for having the courage to admit to my addictions. It meant so much to me at that time. I'd like to thank him.

I went training for ninety minutes at the hotel's gym. I really thought I was going to keep myself fit for when I got back and that I would be able to go straight back into the team! I was deluding myself.

Closer to home I now had the hardest confession of all to make – to tell Lorraine about my one-night stand. It was the toughest thing I have ever done in my life. It was all the worse keeping such a dark secret from her because she was six months pregnant. What a mess! How on earth was I going to break it to her? I was so scared.

How do you tell your wife that you've had a one-night stand after a drink and drugs binge? It was bad enough that I once attacked Lorraine after losing my temper as gambling debts mounted. But I was so appalled by my betrayal of my pregnant wife that I hardly had the courage to confess my shame to her. After all she had been through and then the pain of my going public with all this stuff, I was worried sick what the shock would do to her. The idea was still nagging away that she would walk out on me.

For two days the British public had been reading the details of what I had been doing, while Lorraine had been left in ignorance. She sat white with shock when I finally told her. I felt utterly ashamed about what happened and I told her how sorry I felt. I didn't want to make excuses, but I was high on drugs at the time, I explained. That wasn't the real Paul Merson. I was surprised at Lorraine's reaction. I thought she would be furious with me and I wouldn't have been surprised if she had threatened to throw me out. But after hours of soul-searching, she made the decision I had been praying for. 'I'll stand by you. I'm not going to leave you,' she told me, but I knew how broken-hearted she was inside. She asked me if this meant I would be turning over a new leaf. I told her, 'No – a new life.'

Lorraine told me that this was my last chance, and that she was not going to let me out of her sight again. I was a lucky man. I didn't deserve it, and I was grateful. She wanted us to stay together and try to work it all out. She also said she was glad to be away from all the fuss back home, and anyway I don't think she could have stood all the hassle and attention.

I feel utterly ashamed of what happened, and it will never happen again. It's just not like me. I think the world of Lorraine and the kids, and I feared this latest revelation would break her heart. I'd never look at any other woman unless I was drunk or stoned. But it was clearly better for the story to come out this way than for her to read it in a Sunday newspaper.

That weekend, a Sunday paper printed a story about me, suggesting I'd been with a former Arsenal receptionist. I suppose they thought they could say what they liked about me, but that story was just not true. Fortunately Lorraine now knew the full truth.

Bill was nice to us. He hired a car and drove us around. We were delighted. On one journey back to the hotel, I asked Bill about Bosnia and Serbia. I could never quite grasp all the political intrigue. Bill explained it all, and I told him, 'When I get back I'll explain it all to the lads – they'll think I've been to college!'

My days in Cannes were clearly defined – breakfast, training, running, gym work, lunch, shopping, swimming, trying to get back into shape. I was out to show that my life and career were not going to be over. I wanted to prove that I was not washed up at the age of twenty-six. I promised George Graham I would return in much better shape than when I left. People were happily saying that I was finished, but I refused to accept that. I knew even then that I could kick cocaine. I had already given it up and I had pledged to myself that I would not be taking it again. Instead of sulking, dwelling on the repercussions of what I had done, I tried to look forward. That's why I was working out in the gym, working hard every day.

Delicate negotiations were going on back in London between Highbury and the Football Association. The FA were anxious for me to return quickly for an interview with their senior staff and medical experts. I had been given permission by George to stay away for a week but it had to be cut short. After five days it was time for me and Lorraine to return home and face reality.

It seemed fated that we should move on. All the worry I went through not to be spotted, and then, when we walked into the hotel dining room for lunch, we were confronted by a new intake of guests – an entire group of English tour operators. Naturally enough it wasn't long before I was recognized. Maybe I wasn't a well-known football face before all this, but now my picture was on every back page, and most front pages of the national newspapers back in England. There were a few embarrassed shuffles from fellow guests when they realized who I was and that everyone back home was trying to find me. In England everyone, notably the media, was trying to guess my secret hideaway, hitting on anywhere from Florida to the Spanish Costas.

I got back to England on 29 November and was hauled before the FA on 1 December. The meeting lasted about ninety minutes – the most nerve-racking ninety minutes I'd ever been through. I was glad about their reaction. Present at the meeting were Ken Friar, George Graham, representatives from the FA's specialist drugs unit and medical staff. I broke down when I started to talk about my problems and they must have sympathized because they held back from any lengthy ban. They wanted to rescue my career, not force me out of the game. But at the same time the FA made it very clear that if I returned to drug-taking and my old ways I would have to face the consequences. A ban would have pushed me over the edge.

Graham Kelly, the FA's Chief Executive, explained to me that I would not take the field again until I agreed to an extensive rehabilitation programme, and that they had taken this course of action with the cooperation of the players' union.

The most important thing I wanted to get across to the FA was that I was determined to become a reformed character. I wanted to change my life around. I wanted to play for Arsenal again as soon as I had sorted out my private life. I told them that I believed I was cured of my cocaine habit and that I had been training every day while I was away. I gave everyone assurances that I had no intention of going back to any form of drug abuse. I made it clear at the time that I never took cocaine or any drugs while I was preparing for a game. I never took anything into the dressing-room and I made sure that if I did take cocaine it was at least two or three days away from a game. That's why I never feared I would fail a drugs test after a match. I only ever took drugs as part of my social life outside football.

I even offered to help the FA's fight against drug abuse. And I still want to advise young professional footballers how to avoid getting hooked themselves. I know that teenage stars are at greatest risk. I wanted to open a help-line to give advice, and I still do.

My advice is simple – don't do it. I needed that advice myself but there was no one there to give it to me. I don't want that to happen to youngsters. I owe it to the game to put something back and this is what I want to do. I am prepared to spend as much time as necessary going into youth clubs and the schools to talk to kids even before they go to the clubs. I am sure even after all this there are plenty of people who still idolize me and still look up to me. I know that in particular there are kids who worship me. They'll listen to me so much more than to a social worker or a policeman. It's about time I set the right example. I know that.

But I think people had got the wrong idea. I'm not a junkie and never have been and I loathe it when that's how I'm described. Yes, I had to have cocaine when I was out socially, but I had put a stop to it and it was out of my system by the time I got back to playing.

Later the FA paraded me at a press conference because of the pressure of media interest. I was not used to facing the media and I wasn't looking forward to it. But once it got going, I felt more relaxed, and was in the mood to tell the truth about my condition.

I blurted it out: 'I'm a compulsive gambler, *not* a compulsive drug-taker. I'm not just trying to turn over a new leaf – I'm turning over a new life. I don't sit indoors at night and say, "Right, I've got to have drugs" when I'm sober. But if I am sitting indoors I have to have a bet – and that's why I'm a compulsive gambler.'

I was flanked by Graham Kelly, George Graham and Gordon Taylor. It was decided by the FA's medical advisers that I should be extremely frank about my problems. Everyone described me as having 'a haunted look'. I told the media that I put a lot of my problems down to gambling and using the drug when I went out with others. I'd get drunk and that's when I would use the stuff.

I tried to explain my concerns about the dangers of drugs. You see warnings everwhere about the dangers that cigarettes do – but you don't see anything about what cocaine does. And I was completely ignorant of how much harm it does. Cigarettes give you lung cancer, but you don't see anything about how much damage cocaine can do.

I was fully aware of how many people were convinced that I would slip back into my old ways. But that only served to make me stronger, determined to prove those people wrong. The trouble was that I had a lot of free time on my hands. It was now up to me to spend that time with the family.

In fact I really thought I would be going straight home after that appearance. How wrong I was. I was told I would be going straight to the rehabilitation centre instead. I thought I would only need a couple of days' treatment, but they told me it would be six weeks at least. I can't describe how shocked I was. Nevertheless I did realize that this was my last chance. The FA had been brilliant, the club supportive and my family really understanding. It was up to me now.

The Football Association, the Professional Footballers Assocation and Arsenal issued a joint statement:

'Paul Merson was very frank about his problems. They are considerable. Taking drugs – to which we are all bitterly opposed – is only one of them, and arguably not the biggest. In our view, a complex and unprecedented situation demands that the first priority must be rehabilitation.

– Paul has entered a voluntary agreement to take part in a programme of rehabilitation and treatment at a residential centre chosen by the FA. While there, he will undergo assessment and counselling. Facilities will exist to enable him to maintain fitness under the direction of Arsenal staff.

– He will not be available to play for the club during this period.

– How long this residential programme lasts will be up to specialists and FA medical staff. It is most unlikely though to be less than six weeks.

– This will be followed by a further period of up to 18 months, during which Paul will be monitored and subject to random tests.

– At what stage he returns to competitive football will depend on the agreement of medical specialists, FA officials and his club.

– The financial cost of Paul Merson's rehabilitation will be borne substantially by the player himself.

– If at any stage he fails to comply with a programme designed to help him, disciplinary action will be inevitable.

– The FA looks forward to the day we can take up Paul Merson's offer to work on an anti-drugs programme in schools and elsewhere.

– Meanwhile, tonight with Arsenal and with the PFA, we are all committed to fighting the drugs problem and to helping Paul Merson.'

I really objected to some of the questions suggesting that I only confessed to my addictions to cash in. I made it plain that I did not do it for the money. And I told the FA they could have it all if they wanted it. The money helped pay my rehabilitation costs and part of my gambling debts. I tried to explain the reasons. I thought that if I kept it confidential between the club and the FA, somewhere along the line those people that I'd been involved with in taking cocaine would seek to sell their story. I just felt I had to come out into the open.

The press conference over, Jerome's partner Jeff Weston drove me down to the rehabilitation centre in Southampton. I was frightened and bewildered, unsure of my future, or indeed if I had any future. It wasn't hard to realize I was facing the toughest six weeks of my life.

When I got to Marchwood Priory Hospital I no longer felt like a soccer star. I was the same as everybody else with the same sort of problems. At first I was apprehensive, worried and slow to open up, but in time I was able to talk freely about my innermost thoughts.

The people at the hospital became my new friends and confidants; they were so different from the hangers-on I had been used to who had led me down the wrong path. For six weeks they were my life. The hospital and the therapy sessions took over. I would bare my soul to the group, cry with them, but together our aim was to pull each other through. Along the way we suffered together – depression, anxiety, confusion; they say you even hallucinate, but I didn't.

During treatment there are five steps towards recovery. And that's how I first began to come to terms with my gambling addiction. My therapy was to write things down as part of my step-by-step programme and later to talk about them to the group. It starts with Step 1.

I've lost my self respect on the football pitch, and with my wife and family, because I was always thinking about gambling and my debts. When I came in here Lorraine's mum told her I haven't been right for about three months because every time they would come around to our house I would just watch the sport, as I had a bet on and wouldn't get involved in any conversation.

My wife objects to my mood swings if I have had a bet. If I had lost I would bite her head off, shout at her. If I'm downstairs watching TV, Lorraine would come down and ask if I was going to bed and if I was losing money and in any financial problem. I would throw the remote control across the room and give Lorraine a lot of verbal abuse. At this stage I would go to bed and cry my eyes out. I never did this sort of thing in the early stages, only when I was in real financial trouble.

It was insanity, the gambling, the money worries, the lies, out of control. I couldn't care if I won or lost. I was drinking and slapped Lorraine. Once I started drinking I couldn't stop. I got into trouble at work, a drink-driving charge. When I was drunk I took cocaine. I was taking cocaine with people I didn't even know. My head went, I couldn't concentrate on football, I wasn't worried about the deterioration of my relationship with Lorraine. I put my career on the line. I was losing control altogether.

I lost my self respect by lying all the time. I was so used to lying that it was just another lie. I felt guilty about lying to Lorraine. But when she finds out how much I have lost she would go mad. I used to think, shit, Paul, this is never going to stop, and I would never get out of this routine and the more I told myself this, the more I never felt it would.

I felt totally powerless and unmanageable over my gambling, I couldn't stop. I tried to tell myself to stop but something in me would say 'No, it's all right, you'll get yourself out of this mess it you keep gambling.'

I also lost my self respect when I rang up the bank manager and told him I was buying Lorraine a car and I needed to draw £18,000 out which I owed to a bookie. The bank manager gave it with a promise that I would put it back in a week, when I got my signing-on fee. A week later Lorraine rang up the bank to ask the manager about something and he asked her how the car was? But when Lorraine fronted me up about it I lied so much

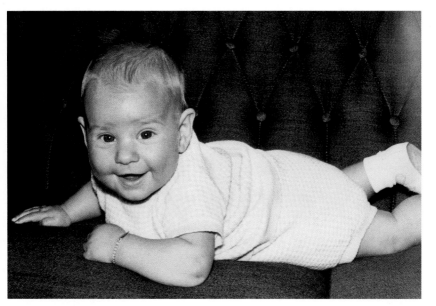

Aged 4¹/₂ months.

Aged 4 weeks, with my nan
(my mum's mum).

With my mum's dad, my brothers, Gary
and Keith, and my sister, Louise.

My dad's mum and dad

My mum and dad.

Training, aged
18 months.

Having a good time with my mum and
sister, Louise

Belmont United under thirteens, winners of the Middlesex Cup.

Aged 12 with my trophies and medals.

Aged 15, dressed up to go to a match at Arsenal.

Nine-year-old goals king

PAUL MERSON is only nine but he is the Brent Schools Under-11 leading striker.

He is a year younger than his team mates who, under manager Alan Jones, are aiming to win four cup competitions—Crisp Shield (London), Bachelor Trophy (Middlesex), Finch Shield (Islington) and the Thames Valley

Schools Soccer
.. every Monday

☐ DEAN WILKINS—brother of Chelsea stars Ray, Steve and Graham—plays for Middlesex Under 16 team against Herts at Owen School, Whetstone, on Saturday (10.30).

Dean plays for Queens Park Rangers' South East

Early press coverage.

Super Paul 'a new Rush'

Paul Merson

By KEN BURGESS

CHARLIE Nicholas reckons wonderkid Paul Merson can save Arsenal a million in the transfer market.

Nicholas h~~ ~~ playing alongside the teenager in the ~~y~~—and he calls the 18-year-old ~~n~~ Rush."

~~aul~~'s a very exciting player. "He's ~~t~~ a good touch, and likes taking ~~~reat runs.

~~~od finisher. He's a nicely gifted ~~~have to teach him much.

." He just needs experience —and he'll get a run this season. Paul reminds me of Rush with the type of runs he makes. He gets in and goes," added Nicholas.

Merson, a six-footer from Ealing, impressed on his only first team appearance, as substitute in the last 15 minutes against Manchester City two weeks ago.

And he starred on TV this

Gunner Merson

By Mike Donovan

EALING & District soccer striker Paul Merson will sign for Arsenal as an apprentice professional this summer.

Marksman Merson, 16 next month, of Farrier Road, Greenford, is to sign in July when he leaves Greenford High School. He has been an associated schoolboy with the first division giants for two years.

He trains every Monday and Thursday and on many Sundays while turning out for the Gunners' youth team in friendly matches. The youngster has also attend~~ed~~

In action against Sheffield United.   *(Photograph: Paul Brooks)*

Just scored against Blackburn. *(Photograph: Tony Edenden, Sports Photo)*

Scoring against Liverpool. *(Photograph: John Davie)*

Meeting Nelson Mandela as Nigel Winterburn looks on, 1993.
(Photograph: Bob Thomas)

Charlie poses with my 1989 Young Player of the Year award and my
Man of the Match trophy from the 1993 Coca Cola Cup final.

16 June 1990.

With Charlie & Lorraine on holiday.

The new me with Lorraine, Charlie, Ben and Sam, July 1995.
(Photograph: Andrea Heselton)

to the bank manager. I told Lorraine the money would be here next week. Of course I was lying, that was another reason why I was powerless and unmanageable over gambling.

My job was going downhill, from once being the main boy on the terraces I became the target of the boo-boys and it didn't really bother me because all I was worried about was to see how my bets got on when I got off the pitch. In training if I hadn't got my bets on before I would just go through the motions in training and be thinking of how much I was going to win. I never thought I would lose even though the day before I could have lost up to £10,000. And that just went on like clockwork for two months.

If there was anything on TV which I was betting on and watching I would just blank the boys and watch TV. Never take them out for the day. If I did I would always be thinking of how my bet was getting on.

I am totally powerless over my gambling and I've realized that because I wouldn't be in here now if I wasn't.

I can no longer gamble safely because I can't control the compulsion. I've tried before and it didn't work... I can't control my thoughts. I can't control my temper. I would lose my wife and kids and job. I would lose my house and be in financial difficulties for the rest of my life.

It means that I have a disease which will not let me bet at all ever again because I will never be able to keep it in proportion. It affects every part of my life.

When me and Lorraine went out with friends at night, if I had a bet on I would be sitting around the table and everyone was talking, but I would be thinking of making an excuse so I could go and use the phone to see how my bet had got on. If it had won I would be soul of the night, but if I lost I would just be sitting there.

Even in these preliminary stages, I set out my goals.

I needed to get my sanity back in my life. I wanted a normal family life again, a much better financial position and wanted to start enjoying my football more. Then, I'll sleep much better because there would be no financial or marriage problem, I'd feel happier, be able to concentrate, relax and care.

It was a painful experience of self-analysis. And it is a battle within myself that I have to win every day, for the rest of my life.

I can close my eyes now and picture a member of my NA group at the Marchwood Hospital during his 'share', when he related his experiences. I can hear his words any time I close my eyes. It's a story that goes right through to my bones. When he told his story, it reminded me of myself. It ran parallel to my life up until the age of twenty-six, but his went forward to a stage which really frightened me to death.

He moved on to crack, heroin and prison.

And I knew that could have been me had I not had treatment – without a doubt. When I heard his story it scared the life out of me because that's where I was heading. I had an addictive personality and cocaine would not have been enough for me. Within a year I would have moved on to something stronger, like crack, and eventually ended up a heroin addict.

Another of the steps was to write out your life story in your own words and then read it out to the group.

And this is my life story. It is not one I have written for this book, and in fact since I've been out of Marchwood Priory I have remembered things that I couldn't recall when I wrote it. What follows is the life story I had to prepare and read to my first therapy group at the hospital. It is a self-cleansing process, a baring of the soul, to be honest with people who can tell at a glance, let alone with a word, whether you are being frank with yourself. It took me forty-five minutes to tell my group my story. I had to prepare it, write it all down, and then read it out in front of everybody. Going from the day I was born up to the worst excesses of my alcohol abuse, it was a vital stage of my therapy. I sat in front of the entire group and went through my entire life story, admitting that I was an alcoholic, 'sharing' my experiences and problems with the rest of the group, as they would have to share theirs with me, as part of the group.

This is a life story that will last for life because it is how it was and is with me and how it will be for the rest of my life.

The pre-school years (1-5 years)

I was born on 20 March, 1968 in Park Royal Hospital, Harlesden, North West London. I'm the oldest of four children which is one sister and two other brothers who from this day get on really well together. My mum is nine years younger than my dad. My mum was a housewife and had part-time jobs when she could get them, but usually she would work from home, and my dad is a coalman and has been for the whole of his life. My mum and dad were quite poor. We lived on the top floor of a house which was small. My dad would always take me down to the park to play football and my dad would always say don't pick the ball up. I was always weeing the bed at this time and I can faintly remember my dad arguing with my mum which frightened me.

(5-12 years of age)

I was becoming a sad boy. This was because I was always coming home from school asking my dad if he was staying in tonight because he would always go out and play cards all night, and my mum would sometimes get me to ring my dad at the card school to see when he was coming home but the man on the phone would say he was not there. But I could hear his voice saying 'tell him I'm not here'. I would be crying in bed. And sometimes my dad would hide me in my mum's bedroom to see where she hid her wages and then he would nick them and go out and gamble it away.

I didn't like school one bit unless we were playing football. I remember my auntie used to cook the school dinners and I never liked eating when I was about seven years old, so I would just sit there. But the headmaster would make me eat it but my auntie would see this from the kitchen so she would come and throw it away and I thought at that stage I could get away with things easy. And on Sunday my mum and dad would let me eat my dinner in the front room while the football was on, but when they were in the other room I would throw my dinner out the window and tell them I had eaten it.

I then found out I had a speech impediment at about five. I couldn't pronounce my s's, so my mum took me every week to a special class.

*My dad would always take me down the park and play football
the day after he'd been out all night and I loved playing football
with him.*

*There was a teacher at my new school who took a liking to me
because I was good at football and he was the games teacher. He
became good friends with my dad and he would give me reading
lessons and I was growing to like school at last because before
that I hated it and all I was interested in was playing football.*

*I was very shy and nervous of school. I would sometimes have
to come off the pitch when I was playing because I got palpitations. I would go dizzy and wouldn't be able to breathe properly.
That would frighten me. Then the summer before I started high
school I had a bad accident playing football and it was touch and
go if I would ever play football again and I was very scared and
frightened about this because at this stage all I wanted to be was
a footballer even though sometimes I wouldn't want to play in a
game. But my dad always made me take part in the game and I
would always be happy he had forced me to go to the game. But
before that I would sometimes be very angry that I had to play
even if I didn't fancy it.*

*I started high school three weeks after everyone else so that
didn't help my shyness and nerves but when I got there I made a
few friends and I settled in well. When I used to watch the school
play football or any sport I would get very angry and unhappy but
always had that belief that I would play football again one day.*
(Teens)

*I was very shy with the girls at school. I was very spotty as
well, but no one would take the mickey out of me because I had
this reputation as being a hard nut even though I wasn't. I think
this was because I was good at football and the school would
look up at me and I would always muck around in class and play
jack the lad with my mates and show off. Because all I wanted to
do was play football I got offered an apprenticeship at Arsenal
just before I left school and that made me feel the happiest boy
in the world. From the age of five I have always wanted to be a
footballer and this was my big chance. It made my mum and dad*

feel very proud and happy. I was so pleased for my dad as well as for myself after all the travelling my dad had done for me, taking me all over the place and taking me over the park.

The summer before I left school I went to Arsenal and when I finally left school I went completely off the rails. I started drinking a lot and then I started smoking dope, which made me feel very tired and shitty but I would always take it because all my friends were, and then I was arguing with my dad because I was staying out all night partying. But I thought I was the dog's bollocks and I wouldn't listen to anyone else.

In that summer I met Lorraine who is now my wife, but at the start of our relationship it was not all perfect. She was still at school and I remember our relationship was touch and go. I remember us all hanging around outside a chip shop and Lorraine went for a walk with a boy from her school and came back five minutes later and I have never forgotten that even though she might have thought we weren't going out with each other. Even now I don't like her going out and I'm very jealous because of what happened ten years ago.

I got engaged to Lorraine at 17 and it was great but then I got in the first team at Arsenal and started hanging around with the big stars at the club and started to go to all the top nightclubs in London. Lorraine didn't like this because I was always out being jack the lad thinking I had made it in the big time. So we split up and I kept drinking a lot and didn't really have time to miss Lorraine because I was always out getting drunk.

Then my game went downhill and a lot of the big stars got thrown out. Lorraine still kept in touch with my mum and dad and so we started going out with each other again and got engaged again. She made me so happy and we set a date for the wedding.

I discovered at the age of 18 that I was a very nervous and shy person, but when I was drunk I had a so-called good personality and was jack the lad. It was an attitude of 'look at me I'm Paul Merson with the bad image.'

From the age of 16 I started to really get into gambling in a big way, always blowing all of my wages for the month on gambling. Sometimes I would do my wages within two hours of getting them out of the bank. When I had no money left I would feel sick and would feel like crying and saying to myself 'never again.' But I never stopped and the more wages I got the more money I gambled away. And, when I lost, it really got me down. I would have a go at Lorraine if she came round my house to see me over any little thing. I would always lie to my mum and dad about my wages, saying that I left them in the bank and that would make me feel guilty and ashamed.

At 17 I played my first game for the reserves which is the team under the first team, and I had to come off because I got palpitations, an attack of despair, couldn't breathe, and went dizzy. So, I went to the doctor and told him about it and he did some tests and said that it is all down to nerves and that if I didn't get over this I would have to pack in football which made me very frightened. But I got over this and since then it's been all right. I've never had to come off again but I sometimes still get it but it always goes very quickly.

(18-25 years old)

At 19 me and Lorraine bought a new house a long way from our mum and dad. The house was right near a pub and I met loads of new friends in the pub, and also became good friends with the landlord, so I always got afters. So, I would always come home from the pub drunk out of my head. some nights I would go over to the pub at 10.50 knowing that I could get afters and get in at about 4 o'clock. This continued for a long time and I felt my drinking getting heavier and heavier and then I did the worst thing when drinking and got done for drink-driving. The club fined me two weeks wages and I went to court and got an 18-month ban. This problem over drink continued and I kept getting into trouble over it. I was banned from the club for two weeks for being louder than the comedian, and then having a fight in the car park. But something in the back of my mind was trying to tell me I was some kind of legend because I had been thrown out of the club for two weeks.

Then I got sent home from Singapore (on Arsenal's end of season tour) for being drunk and throwing a glass ashtray at someone in a night club. When I got sent home with three other lads I still thought it was funny because I thought this would make me stand out to all the others and I was believing what the papers were saying about my bad boy image. I was trying to live up to it. When I got home from Singapore the club fined me another two weeks wages but this didn't seem to stop me. I kept going out and one night I stayed out drinking and playing cards in a pub and pushed Lorraine to the limit because when I came in this particular morning Lorraine was going to work as I was coming in. So I gave her a wave like I had done nothing wrong. I was in the bedroom getting undressed to go to bed, when Lorraine came in and threw a cup of tea over me, but fortunately it missed, and hit the wall. I was too drunk to notice too much and just fell asleep. When I woke up she was painting the wall.

I stopped going out because I then realized what I had been doing to Lorraine and what a wanker I had been. I realized drinking was getting me in trouble a lot of the time and it was costing me money from fines. Then in June 1990 I married Lorraine and it was one of the best days of my life. Having two babies also made me very happy and proud. But then I started gambling heavily on the phone, and it started getting me down because I never seemed to win and I would always have to borrow money off friends and that made me feel very embarrassed and ashamed that I had to loan money off friends who were on nowhere near my wages.

Then, when the kids started sleeping through the night I started to go out again and then started taking cocaine, which I would never have thought of doing. But when I was taking it part of me was saying 'you get caught taking this and you're finished.' But I couldn't stop and the more money I lost on gambling, I would go out and get drunk and snort cocaine, because I would then forget about my gambling debts. But by the time I woke up in the morning I had more problems on my mind because I was then thinking the papers would find out that I was taking drugs. It was getting worse and I was starting to get paranoid and very *frightened of everything that was happening to me and at the end I couldn't handle it because it was getting me down so much. It came to such a pitch that I smashed my bedroom up and ended up in the corner of the bedroom crying my eyes out, frightened like a little sad boy who didn't know what to do. So I just folded up and hoped the earth would eat me up.*

My assets at this time of my life are that if I'm not drunk, gambling or using, I'm a good dad and a lot of people have told me that. I know as well that I am a very kind person. I love buying Lorraine and the kids presents.

(Chemical Dependency)

My addiction was like an on-off addiction. I would go through patches where I would drink and gamble a real lot and then I would switch off and not drink and gamble a lot. I would only have binges on drink and that has been the case since I was 17. But when I do something I have to go the full hog like at the end I wouldn't stop gambling. When I lost what I had I kept going till I was fully in the shit and that has been the case with drinking since I was 17. Once I had one drink I would get drunk out of my head and I can not remember off the top of my head where I've had a drink and not gone on and got drunk. Drinking has been causing big problems since I was 17 and gambling has been causing me problems from about the age of 20 when I had to start borrowing money and that to me is when my gambling became a real problem.

Cocaine has only been a problem over the last four months but to me it has given me just as much problems as drink and gambling even though it has only been a problem for a short time.

Drinking has caused me loads of problems. I've had blackouts where I've woken up in the morning and cannot remember a lot of what has happened. But by the end of the day I would have remembered everything – even if someone had told me what had happened that would trigger it off and then I would remember.

At the end of my nightmare I didn't even have to be drunk to do something silly. I was in such a state that I smashed up the

82

whole of my bedroom by throwing everything all over the floor, smashing the door and smashing the phone. I hurt Lorraine in a big way because I treated her really badly. In the end I used my house like a hotel. I would come in and go out all the time and since I've had the chance to sit down and think about what I was doing I would have hated it to have happened to me, and I've got to make it up to my kids as well because in the end I stopped taking them up to the park and being the dad I used to be to them. Sitting down analysing my life I know deep down this is going to be with Charlie for the rest of his life unless I become a good dad again and give him enough happy days to forget those horrible days that I can remember.

Through drink, gambling and 'using' my football became a nightmare. I was letting myself down in a big way but also it's a team game and I was letting them down as well. I would go out on the pitch and even though I was fit I would be knackered after five minutes of a game because I was mentally tired think-ing about other things. Instead of enjoying my football I used to hate playing and training. That made me feel guilty and ashamed because people would pay their money to watch and I was get-ting good wages and playing badly. I was going through the motions, thinking that if my horse bet had won, I was not too bothered if we won because my heart wasn't in it. That was how the illness was affecting me.

I feel very sad that I treated Lorraine so unthinkingly and very angry with myself that I stopped playing with my little kids and was more worried about other things:

I need to deal with my family life first and start getting my wife to trust me again. I know it's going to be hard but I couldn't live without her and the kids. I've got to get my wife to really love me again because I'm not kidding myself I've hurt her and the kids, especially Lorraine more than she's showing at the moment.

The thing that caused me the most problems, that I would like to make amends, is my jealousy over Lorraine. I'm very jealous about her and I intend to let go and let her live her life normally without me saying anything, and me staying clean and sober. I

*will be much better about this because the only time I would get
jealous was when I was drunk.*

*To maintain my recovery I will have to talk a lot on the phone
to my sponsor and go to AA and GA meetings and a few NA meetings in between because I've made my mind up that I'm going to
make GA and AA my main two meetings because looking back
I only took cocaine when I was drunk. I must also get phone
numbers from people I can trust and also keep in touch with the
group when we leave because they've been a big help to me.*

Those people at Marchwood have become my best friends, and
we are still in constant touch. They know me better than anyone
else in the world. You come to trust people. I really had to open
myself up – it's all about trust. The first few days it was, 'I can't
tell you this, I can't tell you that.' But you come to trust people
and I'd share anything with those people. In there I was an alcoholic, I wasn't a footballer, and everybody treated me the same,
which was good. I can't forget I'm a professional footballer, but
I'm still an alcoholic – so I've got to confront that.

As I said earlier, George Graham had given me quite a few 'last
chances'. But I knew this was the final one. The 'boss' had made
that perfectly plain. Although I had been nothing but a source of
frustration to him, he gave me tremendous understanding – and
plenty of patience. I leaned particularly heavily on him when the
media reaction was mixed. It was tough when people such as former England and Spurs player and QPR manager Alan Mullery
advocated a life ban. But Alan Hansen, in his *Today* column,
showed a great deal of understanding.

Another very important aspect of my life at this time was the
support of Arsenal. Chairman Peter Hill-Wood spoke out in my
favour. I was so heartened when he publicly said: 'The boy is in
a mess. His career is in disarray. But Arsenal are not going to
throw the book at him. Merson has gone beyond that kind of
punishment. What is the point in us fining or suspending him?
Paul has got to take a long hard look at himself. What he is about,
where he is going. We all know what would happen if we kicked
him out. He has lost control of himself. He has reached the edge

of the cliff. If he goes over the top his career is over. Then there would be nothing we nor anyone else could do for him. I can think back to the 30's when players with talent wasted it. He is the latest. Nothing changes. He does not have a particularly high intelligence and is unable to cope with the fame and fortune that football has brought him. If he wants to fight back then we can help him. He needs help quickly. He has to kick the habit. He also needs mental help. I believe that he needs to see a psychiatrist. He needs to be counselled. Somewhere inside Paul is a smashing boy. But he is unable to cope with the fame and fortune football has brought him. It is a sad story. I have never known somebody with such expression as a footballer yet lacking such self-confidence as a person. It is a complex mix. It is true that at board level we have discussed Paul's behaviour over the years. There have been incidents which we have not liked. But not once has it been discussed to kick him out of the club. That is not Arsenal's way. And manager George Graham has always been supportive of him. He knows, like us, that here is a world-class talent. A cult figure with our fans. A player who can be so good. He is worth fighting for. Now he has made perhaps the hardest decision of all. He has come clean. Now it is up to him to prove that he can fight back completely. Because Paul knows, football knows, that this is his last chance. And he must do it without the wrong people around him. It is no secret that Paul has mixed with the wrong sort of person over the years.

'What has happened is awful. But it has happened. It is no good us trying to hide. We are here to help him. But at the end of the day he can only help himself. The trouble is he's so inconsistent. After a few minutes of a game you can tell if he's in the mood – or you know he was on the booze the night before. Now it is up to him to prove he can fight back completely, because Paul knows this is his last chance.'

I suppose some people might have taken some of Peter Hill-Wood's comments the wrong way, especially his remark about me 'not having a particularly high intelligence'. I think it was a good comment. I agree with it. He was perfectly entitled to say that, because at that time I was acting like a complete idiot, with sub-normal intelligence.

I had been overjoyed by the support of Arsenal fans. At Highbury at 3.18 p.m. on the Saturday after my confession, the supporters spontaneously burst into song: 'There's only one Paul Merson.' It echoed around the stadium. My dad told me on the phone when I rang from France and it made me feel so good.

Trevor Brooking, on the other hand, believed I should have suffered a long ban and he made his thoughts known on BBC's *Match of the Day*.

'I have a certain sympathy with Paul – it's a great shame for an individual with exceptional talent, but it's an even greater shame for the game. Cannigia and Maradona have been banned and I feel that Merson should have the same long-term suspension to act as a deterrent. That target has to be young players, and the FA has to make sure they clamp down. Unfortunately that must mean for Paul Merson a long suspension.'

I was shocked that there was any suggestion that I'd be banned. I hadn't brought the game into disrepute – I'd brought myself into disrepute. It's something I regretted deeply and wanted to do something about. I didn't think I had hurt the game of football. That was certainly never my intention and something I would never do. I've hurt myself and my family more than I've hurt the FA.

But I felt intense pressure when some MPs insisted I should face prosecution, so I was so relieved that Arsenal decided that they wouldn't stop my wages just at a time when I needed the money to pay off my debts. Had they disciplined me I would have gone deeper into debt. It wasn't easy when I read in the papers that if I was charged and found guilty of possessing cocaine I could face a prison sentence of up to seven years.

A week before I was discharged from the hospital, I was summoned to a consultation with medical experts from the FA, and the club, at a place that everyone wanted to keep quiet so as to prevent the media turning up. I went back to the hospital a few hours later. The idea was that reports would be sent to the

FA, who would have the ultimate say on when I would be able to leave – and when I would be able to play again.

I was so delighted when I was told that the reports were favourable. The FA had been told that I had made enormous strides, but I would have to resume training with Arsenal, and then await a final assessment before I could play. The boss wanted me back as soon as he could, as results were not too good and he was under increasing pressure.

On Friday 13 January I was finally released. Stephen Stephens told me in the middle of a therapy session that morning that I had an hour to pack and get ready to go.

7

A NEW BEGINNING

FRIDAY 2 DECEMBER
Jeff Weston drove me down to the hospital. I was very anxious
about what to expect when I got here. When I got here I talked
to the doctor and had a big cry when I was told I might not be
able to go home and see my wife and kids for Christmas. Then, I
got shown around the hospital. I was thinking, shit, how can I
get out of here? I went to my room which was like a rabbit hutch.
I got introduced to a man called John, who went running every
day. So we arranged to go running in the morning. When I went
to bed that night, I just lay in bed and cried my eyes out like a
little boy and said to myself 'what the fuck have you done with
your life?' I was frightened and scared.

SATURDAY 3 DECEMBER
Got up early and went for a run with John, which I find very
hard, because of all that has happened in the past couple of days.
I had my first session of therapy and watched TV with John and
Jack. There was an article in the paper about me going to prison
about my cocaine confession which me and Lorraine were very
worried about. But she rang the police and they said that there's
nothing to worry about, so that was a big relief off my shoulders.
So now I can really concentrate on my therapy and get better
and become the husband that my wife married. I sit in my room
tonight thinking what am I going to do with my life. I lay in bed
frightened and scared of what is to come and can I handle it or
will I throw everything away.

SUNDAY 4 DECEMBER

Me and Lorraine read another newspaper article which she was
very upset about but like usual she just shrugs it off and gets on
with life and shows how strong she is, and one of my aims while
I'm in here is to come out of here into the real world as strong
as she is. I went with John on another run which I found a bit
easier because he went slower! Rang Lorraine to talk to Charlie
and Ben and she said 'don't worry what's in the paper' and that
made me feel good. I watch TV with John and Jack all day and
listen to the radio because John wanted to see how Stoke got on.
They lost 1-0 and he was pissed off so I took the mick out of him.

I was allowed out tonight with John to the sweet shop.

It felt good to be allowed out after just two days because you've
got to be in at least a week before you're allowed out. But because
I was with John they let me go.

I cried my eyes out to Lorraine again on the phone. I just
keep on thinking about not going home for Christmas, because
Christmas is the best time of the year for me, just to see the boys'
faces when they open their presents and when they used to leave
Santa a mince pie and a Budweiser because I said he drank beer
– but the drink was really for me.

MONDAY 5 DECEMBER

I've enjoyed today because I learnt a lot about what I've got to
expect in my five steps I've been told I have got to do in here.

The police are coming down to interview me about my cocaine
confession tomorrow and I feel very nervous and frightened. But
I've been told not to worry from other people but that's easy for
them to say.

I had to fill out alcohol and drugs assessments today and tell
what my drink and drugs days were like. Been given my books
today. One of them is an NA book to tell me about drugs and
what they do to you.

Group was good today. I told the group I was pissed off with
not doing GA sheets at dinner but when I got back to my room
and thought about it, I realized I shouldn't be pissed off and let

Steve and Jeanette help me because they are my counsellors and they know what they are talking about.

Now I'm going to watch TV with the rest of the group in the TV room which I have nicknamed The Betting Shop because they all smoke like mad.

Again I've talked to Lorraine on the phone and she's talking about how she was a bit worried taking Charlie to school this morning but she said she would because she's got to face them sooner or later, and tonight when I talked to her she said everyone was great at the school and Charlie's teacher Mrs Irwin was brilliant and Lorraine showed me again how strong she is and that I've got to learn how to be that strong. Because every day I talk to her she makes me stronger and I realize how stupid I've been before I came in here.

Didn't go running with John this morning because my Achilles was hurting but the rest of the group took the mickey out of me and said I bottled it!

TUESDAY 6 DECEMBER
Today's been a really hard day.

I have had my interview with the police and they were very understanding and gave me a caution which I was very pleased with. But I must admit it was a very frightening experience. I went through so many different emotions, because now it's all over the fear has changed to relief. Thankfully it is all over, but despite the worry it didn't make me want to have a bet, drink or take drugs.

In my hospital 'daily diary', under the section 'today I feel I have made good progress in the following areas', I wrote: 'I have been given step 1 and I kept my sanity about me after the interview.'

The other thing today was that I was told I was an alcoholic and addicted to drugs after I filled out the assessment on Saturday. This frightened me to know that I was both of these, because after all this time I never knew. I rang Lorraine and told her that I was both of these and she seemed very shocked but after a few seconds she said if you think about it you are an alcoholic because the way I used to drink so soon as I had had one drink I couldn't stop and if I ever went out for a drink I would not come home till I was drunk or the last place had closed.

I was given Step 1 today on gambling, drink and drugs and I have to have it ready by Monday morning.

After dinner I asked the lady for a sharp knife to peel my apple but she said I was not allowed and she took the apple and peeled it in the kitchen. That made me feel very angry.

I went to the aftercare meeting in the evening where all the other people who have been in treatment came back for. After the meeting I realized that you don't have to have a drink to enjoy yourself.

WEDNESDAY 7 DECEMBER

Today's been a funny day because I'm still trying to come to terms that I'm an alcoholic because when I came in here I knew I had a big problem with gambling but I never really looked at my drinking even through all the trouble I have been in since I've been drinking. I always thought that an alcoholic was someone that drunk every day but if I was injured I would drink every day but if I wasn't I could go a week without a drink. It was very rare if I could go any longer because as soon as I had one I had to have as many as I could. I always said to David Seaman if I cannot get drunk I wouldn't even bother having a drink, and he used to think I was always messing around.

I heard today that Hi-Tec are going to stand by me after we've had a chat to tell them my plans when I get out and play again, which is great news and that makes me feel very happy to know that a big company like that are hopefully going to stand by me.

Everyone tells me in here to do it for myself but I'm not – I'm in here for my family because I love them so much.

In my hospital 'daily diary' report I ringed 'Very Good' for the day I had, and explained: 'I think I helped John about his phone call to his dad, because I could relate to that from my betting on the phone. The phone is the easy way out to have a bet or say something personal, just like what John had said to his dad.'

Under the section 'today I learned', I wrote: 'That I have a higher power in GA and AA and that I learned from the AA meeting in the group room that if you don't do a good step 4 you have a bigger chance of failure.' In the section 'today I enjoyed', I said: 'Going in the AA meeting and listening to everyone's problems and seeing if I can relate to them.' 'Today I did not enjoy': 'watching football because I really miss it but I know that I have to get better first before I can enjoy it like I used to.'

'I am aware of the need to make progress in the following areas': 'To go to as many GA, AA, and NA meetings that I possibly can.'

'I intend to make this progress by': 'Working hard and telling the truth.'

'Other things I felt about today are': 'That I don't want to be the man my wife married because I was still gambling, and drinking then, but I want to be the man I want to be so I can be happy and if I'm happy my wife and kids will be happy. I'm looking forward to my NA meeting tomorrow and I hope I can get as much feed back as I can, as I do at AA.'

THURSDAY 8 DECEMBER
'Today I enjoyed': 'My first NA meeting. Met some really nice people there and especially one who I could really relate to.'

'I am aware of the need to make progress in the following areas': 'That I have to go to as many rooms as I can and to listen and talk.'

'I intend to make this progress by': 'By phoning someone from NA and asking where the next NA meeting is because you can also talk about drink as a drug.'

'Other things I felt about today are': 'That I really realize that I was powerless and unmanageable about drink, gambling and drugs.'

FRIDAY 9 DECEMBER
Today has been an up-and-down day.

For the first time since I've been in here I really wanted to go home. But I rang Lorraine and she talked me around.

I talked to Charlie on the phone this afternoon and he started to cry and say 'when are you coming home daddy', and that really made me feel sad.

John left today and even though I've only known him a week I'm going to miss him because since I've been in here he has been a big help. Thanks John.

I had my first visitors today. Neil and his little boy Daniel came to see me and I was really pleased and that tells me what a great friend he is.

Nigel Winterburn rang today and so did Perry Groves and that makes me feel really good. I talked to Nigel about what's happening at the club and it brought back some memories and that I'm missing football.

I made a couple more friends at the hospital but another went home today and I just hope he's all right outside in the real world again.

In my 'daily diary' form I ringed 'Very Good' and said it was because 'I got a lot of emotions in Jeanette's office when I was talking about drink, gambling and drugs and coming to terms with them.'

'Today I learned': 'That I have a big drink problem and that I am powerless and unmanageable over drink and gambling.'

I felt pissed off and just wanted to go home for a space of half an hour but my group calmed me down and then I felt all right. For the second, 'today I learned' I wrote: 'That if you have got a problem with your work just ask someone about it and don't be embarrassed.'

SATURDAY 10 DECEMBER
Today's been the best day since I've been here. Charlie and Ben came down to see me with my mum and dad. It was really great to see them. We played football in the corridor and then Charlie and Ben changed so we played Power Rangers and then hide and seek. It was great fun and I enjoyed it so much. I've only been in

here just over a week and the boys are really growing up quick. My mum and dad said they haven't seen me look this good for a long time which was great to hear.

Lorraine rang and has had all her hair cut off and I can't wait to see it, but most of all I can't wait to see Lorraine tomorrow because I love her so much and I've missed her so much.

Bouldy (Steve Bould) rang today and we had a good chat, and he said he wanted to come down and see me with Nigel and Ray (Parlour) during the week so I told them that I'll ring Perry and see when he can come down so we can have a little reunion.

It's another day without a bet or drink and I feel really great about that because before that I didn't think I could go out with Lorraine and friends on a Saturday night for a meal without having a drink, but that's all going to change now and I have to learn to socialize without having a drink and the way I feel now I know I can. And get back to playing the way I was when the fans loved me.

There were a lot of tears when Charlie and Ben went home and Charlie didn't want to go but when he left I went back to my room and cried my eyes out, but then talked to my group and they made me feel better.

SUNDAY 11 DECEMBER

Had a lay in this morning and got up at 10.30 because I haven't had so many late nights in a week before. Lorraine came down to see me today with her mum and dad, and my sister Louise. We had lunch in the canteen and then had a great chat in my room about everything. I've missed Lorraine so much and I just want to get home, but first I have to come to terms with my addictions. Me and Lorraine talked about Charlie's birthday next Sunday. After she talked to my doctor, Mr Austin Tate, about me being able to go home for Charlie's birthday and for Christmas he said that he'll have to see about Charlie's birthday but I will be allowed home on Christmas Eve till Boxing Day which made me and Lorraine really happy. Lorraine and the family left about 4.30 and I felt gutted that I couldn't go to Charlie's birthday, but at least I can go home for Christmas.

Lorraine gave me the papers. One had another article in about me. I just wonder when they are going to leave me alone and let me, Lorraine, and the kids get on with our new life. Gary Lewin rang up to see how I was which was nice of him and we talked about tomorrow's game against Man City which I will be able to listen to on the radio.

One week gone and if the other five weeks go this quick I'll be home before I know it.

The boss has just rang to see how I was and to say that he's going to try and come down in the week to see me. I cannot talk highly enough about the boss, how much he's stood by me in all my troubles I've been in at the club. Thank you, boss.

PS. Thanks Lorraine for doing all my washing and ironing for me, I can't believe what a diamond wife I've got. It shows just how messed up I was when I came in here, not to notice in the last two months.

MONDAY 12 DECEMBER

Today has been a really good day. I passed Step 1 of my five-step programme which the rest of the group said is the hardest, because you have to tell the rest of the group everything you have done bad before you come in here. The joy, pain, relief of doing Step 1. I asked if I could talk my Step 1 instead of writing it down and they let me because I'm not very good at writing. Now I've passed I can go out of the hospital on my own now for a run which is really good to know. I went running today and I find it really hard because my Step 1 was very emotional and it took a lot out of me.

The papers are having a go at the boss again, but he's strong enough to look after that and he's got a great club behind him, because I should know for everything they've done for me. He'll bounce back and win a trophy and show the press what I already know, that he's a great manager. I rang Bouldy today at the hotel to wish the team all the best before tonight's game against Man

City, and he said that some of the lads will come down and see me next Tuesday which I'm looking forward to. Wrighty rang this morning and was his usual happy self which is what I've got to hear when people ring me up because they got to remember I'm not in the real world and they have to realize I'm missing it out there but I don't want to come out of here till I'm really ready because I don't want to go back to how I was before.

Lorraine's going out tonight with a few friends and I'm really pleased because what she's been through in the last two weeks is unbelievable and that's the only word I can use to explain it.

I listen to the game on the radio and the lads played really well, great result for the lads and the boss because they needed that result to get the press off their backs.

TUESDAY 13 DECEMBER
Today's been quite a funny day. I went running this afternoon with two ladies down on middle court which probably means you're in for some kind of depression or you're drying out. I thought they would be good runners because that's what they told me, so I knocked on their door and said are you ready. They were sitting there having a fag, so I said I'd wait outside while they got ready, thinking they were going to put their track suits and trainers on. But they just came out with their shoes on and one had her handbag with her as well. I thought they were fooling about. I'm looking to go for a four mile run! Anyway we go outside and started running. I thought they're not bad but by the time we got to the end of the path, which is about 500 yards, they were both knackered. We had to walk the rest of the way to the village where we bought six almond cakes of which one ate four on the way back. The other bought a Mr Man lolly and ate that on the way back with a fag in the other hand. We walked all the way back so it was the easiest day's training I've ever done!

Went to an AA meeting tonight which was very good as I talked about my drink problem.

John came back today to see me and looked really well (good lad). Rang 'Winkie' (Steve Jacobs, my GA sponsor) tonight to see how he was and we talked about how I was and about how I'm doing without a bet because Winkie took me to GA and I need to talk to people who understand me because Winkie's been there before and his wife Mandy can also help Lorraine and they are becoming very good friends and being in here I know I need friends like Winkie and Mandy and not a lot of the mates I had before I came in here because they don't understand my addictions.

WEDNESDAY 14 DECEMBER

It's been another good day today. I played tennis with Dr Tate's wife. We played doubles with two lovely people. Me and my partner won 7-5, 5-5 but we had to stop because I had to come back so I could shower and get ready for my AA meeting which was not very good tonight. I couldn't relate to the man who was sharing his experiences.

I was told tonight that the press know where I am but I don't mind, because I was expecting them to find me early .

I was told by my accountant Steve Smith that Hi-Tec are definitely keeping me on my contract which is very pleasing to hear.

One of the group members Sarah has been unwell tonight so the rest of the group went in and had coffee and a good chat. My group are a great bunch of people. One lady told her life story and we had a good cry.

It's coming towards the weekend and I hope the rest of the group vote that I can go shopping on Saturday and go home on Sunday for my little boy Charlie's fourth birthday party.

THURSDAY 15 DECEMBER

Another good day. Went to an NA meeting and the man that 'shared' told a great story about himself. I've become good friends with one of the NA members called Jamie. We seem to have a lot in common and he seems a great lad. A lady joined the group today and I thought she was a plant from the press so I wouldn't say anything during the group meeting and I fronted her in her room. She said she didn't even know who I was (egg on face). Really she was just as screwed up as the rest of us.

Jack is leaving tomorrow. I'm going to miss him because he's a great man and it means I'm going to be in the group with three women and myself.

One of the counsellors in the rehabilitation centre came to the hospital tonight to ask if I wanted to go training with his team on Tuesday nights to keep fit. Had a long workout with a man who is the second funniest man in the world bar my dad's mate Dick.

Charlie's got an infected ear and me and Lorraine hope that he is going to be all right for his birthday party on Sunday, and I hope that I'll be allowed home. Roll on the weekend so I can see Lorraine and the boys again.

Love you Lorraine, Charlie and Ben xxx.

FRIDAY 16 DECEMBER

It's been a mixed day so far because I am writing at the moment and it's only 4 p.m. We've just come out of group where the subject was to tell everyone what you think of them. And, they said I didn't trust them and that I was childish. The trust bit made me very angry because in my Step 1 I told them virtually everything about myself. But the childish one is true because if I wasn't I wouldn't be bothered what everybody else was doing or worrying what people are saying about me.

The good news is that my Step 2 got passed and that I was told that I can go home for the weekend on Saturday and that means I can go to Charlie's birthday, which really means a lot to me. I rang Lorraine up and told her and I could feel the happiness from her voice.

Talked to Gary Lewin (Arsenal physiotherapist) and Bouldy today about things and Bouldy told me that Paul Davis rang me yesterday and made me feel really good because I look up to Davo because deep down I've always wanted to live the life he does where he gets on with his life with his lovely girlfriend Hope and now their little baby and doesn't worry about being jack the lad like me and trying to be the main boy. I'm always frightened of missing out and worrying about all the other lads and what they think of me.

Today I've been told by my doctor that the Sunday *People* have been on the phone and are going to print a story about me being here.

'Bothered'.

SATURDAY 17 DECEMBER

I've been let out into the real world today. I went home for the weekend. Lorraine's dad picked me up from the hospital at one o'clock after my AA meeting. Me and Stan had a long chat on the way back, about how well I look and talked about how I feel about never having another alcoholic drink. I told him that I had come to terms with that and I have to take it one day at a time.

Lorraine and the boys were really pleased to see me especially the boys because Lorraine didn't tell them I was coming home so when I pulled up in the car the boys went mad with excitement. We played hide and seek this afternoon and I told Charlie and Ben that we would go to the park and play football in the morning after Charlie had opened his birthday presents.

Me and Lorraine had a lovely Indian take-away because in the hospital the food's really nice but I don't get my favourite foods like Chinese and Indians.

Me and Lorraine had a long chat about things and we are much closer now than ever before and just looking forward to the rest of our lives together with the kids.

Rang Jackie from the group at the hospital to see how she was because the rest of the group have all gone home for the weekend, and to see how she's getting on with her Step 1.

Good luck Jackie.

SUNDAY 18 DECEMBER

First full day at home for two weeks.

Got up this morning and me and Lorraine gave Charlie his birthday presents. Just to see the happiness on his face made my weekend. Played football with Charlie and Ben all morning. We all had our Arsenal kit on.

We had Charlie's birthday party at the local hall which was great fun, and Charlie loved every minute of it with all the other children.

Came back home and had a lovely curry which Lorraine cooked for me before I went back to the hospital. Neil picked me up at 6.30 and I headed back down to the hospital in Southampton for another week of therapy.

Had a long chat with Mr Friar (Arsenal chief executive) today when he rang my house to see how I was. I asked how our boss was getting on. He wished me 'good luck'. He said that the doctors had told him that I was doing really well. It's been a great weekend and I can't wait for next week because it's Christmas day.

Thanks for ringing Mr Friar.

MONDAY 19 DECEMBER

Really hard day because the group therapy was really heavy – with loads of tears in the whole group. Eddie Cool, my room-mate, rang today and it was nice to hear from him. Lorraine rang to say that my accountant had sorted out my taxes and debts and now I've paid them all off and I've got a clean slate, which is great to hear when I've been in the shit for so long. Gary Lewin rang and said him, Stewart (George Graham's Number Two Stewart Houston) or Ricey (Pat Rice, member of the back room staff) will be down by the end of the week to give me a really hard training session for an hour, which believe it or not was good news because I've been training on my own bar once over the last week and it's quite boring.

I was given Step 3 today and I've got to present it on Friday. Fingers crossed it gets accepted.

Two more new people joined the group today, one of them is younger than me, but it looks like we are going to get on well because we have a lot in common with each other.

Made a snowman tonight with Sarah and Jackie from a big

traffic cone which we put cotton wool around, put a scarf on and a bobble hat, doggie biscuits for buttons. Then we put decorations up on the wall of our floor. Better not tell Lorraine or I'll have to put them up every year at home! Only messing about Lorraine.

TUESDAY 20 DECEMBER
Another good day.

Played tennis in the afternoon with my doctor's wife, Joan, and played mixed doubles. Score, 6-7, 7-5. So, still unbeaten while I've been in hospital. It was a bit worrying for me when I played tennis because there was a lot of little kids there and, at that age, they are always so honest. I thought they'd blank me and say 'look there's that druggie Paul Merson'. But they were as good as gold and said 'look there's Paul Merson', and they said hello and that made me feel very good. 'Thanks lads.'

I was so pleased that Lorraine enjoyed herself at the theatre with her mum when she went to watch *Oliver*. That made me feel very happy because she has been through so much and when I get out of here I'm going to make it up to her because she's the best thing that has ever happened to me, and that makes me work that much harder so I never want to go back to what I had become because if I did I would lose the most important thing that means the most to me in life, and that's Lorraine, Charlie, Ben and my little baby on the way.

I LOVE YOU LORRAINE, CHARLIE AND BEN XXX.

WEDNESDAY 21 DECEMBER
Today I learned that my little boys could get the disease that I've got. That frightened me a lot because there is no way I want them to go through what I've been through with gambling, drinking and cocaine. That makes me even more determined to get control of this disease so I can be clean and sober just in case they do get a problem over gambling, drinking and drugs because if I go back to how I was I would be no help at all to them or to myself.

Lorraine visited 'Winkie' and Mandy tonight to talk about my gambling problem which is good for Lorraine to understand why I gamble, because 'Winkie' was in the same boat as me and I hope he don't mind me saying but he hasn't had a bet for eight years and like the good friend he is becoming he has said he will help as much as he can and I really appreciate that. And Mandy will help Lorraine because she's been in the same boat as Lorraine and she can understand how Lorraine feels. Thanks 'Winkie' and Mandy.

YOU'LL BE ALRIGHT CHARLIE & BEN. XX.

SATURDAY 24 DECEMBER

Christmas Eve, the day I've been waiting for is here and I'm allowed home. Packed my stuff last night, went to group and then went to the AA meeting in the treatment centre. My friend Neil is picking me up at one o'clock after the meeting. The meeting was brilliant. The man who was 'sharing' his experiences was over from America to visit and came to the meeting. He talked about drink and cocaine and I could relate to a lot of what he was saying.

Neil came at one o'clock and I said to the group 'have a lovely Christmas'. On the way home I went to Brent Cross shopping centre with Neil to get Lorraine some presents. But whatever I buy her, it will never be enough because she is priceless to me. I bought her a few Landro models which she collects and a couple of pairs of shoes from Russell & Bromley, and a handbag. Went home, and saw the kids, who were over the moon to see me. Bathed the kids and then put Father Christmas a mince pie and a glass of milk out. That was a bit different for Charlie and Ben because I used to put out a mince pie and a Budweiser because that's what I told the boys Father Christmas wanted when I was drinking. Stayed in tonight with Lorraine and her mum and dad because last year me and Lorraine went out with friends and I got drunk as usual and woke up with a big bad headache.

GREAT TO BE HOME WITH LORRAINE AND THE KIDS.

SUNDAY 25 DECEMBER

Up before the kids. When they woke, I went downstairs to watch them open their presents in the play room. It was great to see their faces because three weeks ago I would never have dreamed of sitting in my own home watching the kids opening their presents.

I felt like crying one minute and smiling the next.

It was so emotional for me, mum and dad, my brothers, Keith and Gary, who had come over for Christmas.

Mr Friar rang this morning to wish me and Lorraine a Happy Christmas and that means a lot to me for someone to put themselves out to ring me. So thanks Mr Friar.

Lorraine cooked a lovely turkey and the house was dry with no drink after dinner. I tidied up the kitchen and dining room and then played with the kids and their new toys. Rang the rest of the group to see how they were and to wish them a Happy Christmas. The kids had a bath and went to bed and then my mum, dad and brothers went home. Sat down and watched TV with Lorraine and said I wasn't looking forward to going back but she said I had to and I agreed. It's lucky for me Christmas day fell on a Sunday because otherwise I wouldn't have been allowed home.

The group voted that I could come back tomorrow morning, so me and Lorraine chatted about what a great day it was and how much we love each other and then went to bed after a great day.

SO THAT'S WHY I CRIED MY EYES OUT ON 25 DECEMBER.

(In my 'Week's End Diary' report I circled 'very good' for this week. The reason was simple enough as I filled out the form: 'I was allowed home for Christmas to spend it with the family and my Step 3 got accepted.' Under the section 'this week I learned', I wrote: 'That if you relapse it is 1000 times worse than the first time and that you will die if not straight away, it will only be after a matter of time.'

In the section 'this week I enjoyed', I wrote: 'Watching my little boys wake up in the morning looking so excited to see what Father Christmas had got them and when they had opened them to play and to see them really happy and that made me feel happy and proud.'

In the section 'this week I did not enjoy', I wrote: 'Leaving my wife and kids to come back here. It made me feel very sad but I have to come back to get better, and Lorraine understands that so that makes me feel a little bit better.'

The next section is 'this week I feel I have made progress in the following areas'. My notes read: 'That I'm sharing my feelings more and writing them down in my diary more as well.'

'I am aware of the need to make progress in the following areas': 'To keep on phoning people and sharing more at meetings.'

'I intend to make progress by': 'Phoning at least one person a day if not two, not including my sponsor.'

'Other things I felt about this week are': 'That so many people on the outside do not understand this disease. When I'm telling them about me, that I will never be able to drink again or I'll die, they just look at me like I'm an idiot and that pisses me off. But Lorraine says don't even bother telling them because at the end of the day, as long as I know the score, that's all that matters.'

MONDAY 26 DECEMBER

Had to be up early to get back to treatment, and be in group by nine o'clock. Lorraine's dad drove me down to Southampton, leaving at about 6.30 a.m. to make sure I was there for breakfast and in time to get unpacked for another week of therapy. When I left the kids were asleep. I felt very sad and didn't want to leave them. On the way down I was very quiet. I was gutted that I had to leave the kids after such a great weekend.

Went to group and talked about my weekend and then all of a sudden I broke out in tears.

All I could see was the kids asleep in bed when I left.

I calmed down and then carried on with the group. Rang Lorraine after group and then talked to Charlie who said he was crying when he woke up because I wasn't there. That made me feel sad, but then I told him that I'll be home soon and that I love him.

In the evening we had a 'karaoke' in the betting shop (TV room) which was great fun because even when I was drunk I could never sing so it just shows that you can enjoy yourself without a drink.

FRIDAY 30 DECEMBER
Went home New Year's Eve but they didn't want me to. I said I wanted to and I promised that I wouldn't go out of the house.

SUNDAY 8 JANUARY
Filled in my Hospital bulletin diary. 'I went home for the weekend and played with the kids. Went out with Lorraine and went training and enjoyed the whole weekend very much.' I had to write out what I had learned and said 'that I was not ready to go out to a restaurant, not because of the drink, but I was nervous about the other diners, so I said no and we went around to my sponsors and got a take-away.' I had to say why I enjoyed the week and I wrote: 'The meal we had at my sponsors over the weekend, and the chat me and Lorraine had, we got a lot out of it. Lorraine got a few things off her chest and is going to GamAnon on Monday with my sponsor's wife.'

What didn't I enjoy? Well, that was easy, the papers saying that the FA had said that when I leave treatment it wouldn't mean I could play football straight away. I would have to wait till they were ready and that frightened me because I want to get back straight away because if not I will have loads of time on my hands.

I felt I had made progress because, as I wrote in my hospital notes: 'When I didn't want to go to the restaurant I said "no" and I didn't say yes just to please. That made me feel very happy.' The lesson was clear to think before I say yes all the time and to watch my anger.

THURSDAY 12 JANUARY
Was told that the FA will let me know tomorrow if I'm allowed out and whether they can get the press conference all set up. If they can't my doctor told me that they want me to stay in over the weekend because the press had got a sniff that I was coming out

and that they would be around my house. I felt very depressed because I used to love going home for the weekend and being told that I'll have to stay in over the weekend because all the rest of my group were going home on Friday and that I'll be in here on my own and it is quite boring over the weekend.

I rang Lorraine and told her I might have to stay in here over the weekend and I felt very sad but Lorraine said don't worry and we agreed that Lorraine wouldn't come down on Sunday with the kids if I have to stay in because she wouldn't want to take the kids away from me. The first time Charlie and Ben came down with my mum and dad, they didn't want to leave me and there were a lot of tears.

Went to the AA meeting in the treatment centre and 'shared' about my feelings and that made me feel better, and that enabled me to get to sleep that night.

FRIDAY 13 JANUARY

The day I left the treatment centre is a day I'll never forget.

I cried in front of the nation.

I just couldn't stop myself from crying, the sheer pain and joy just overwhelmed me and I just broke down.

From the first moment that I woke the only thing on my mind was the phone call from the FA to my counsellor letting him know if I can go home. Went to my group and at about 10.30 Stephen Stephens came into the room and told me to get ready and pack because I had to be out of the treatment centre at 11.15. I felt great, happy and overjoyed. Said goodbye to everyone for today because those people are such great friends and are one big part of my recovery.

Drove to a neighbour's house to put my suit on, which Lorraine had dropped off because there were a lot of pressmen around my house because they hadn't been told there was going to be a press conference.

Went to the hotel for the press conference and had a cup of tea and talked about how I felt and Mike Parry (FA press officer) was telling me what kind of questions they are likely to ask and

I was wondering how I was going to answer them. But Steve Stephens just said that I should say how it was and be like I was when in treatment sessions, and be honest.

When I went out in front of all of those pressmen and cameras I thought I was all right. But when one man asked me what was it like in there I just cracked up from the relief and what I had been through and how hard it was. As I told them when I was able to talk again, it was the hardest six weeks of my life.

I'll never forget when I cried, the boss held my leg and talked for me. It just showed me again that he has a soft side and he's not just the hard disciplinarian that the press made him out to be.

I would like to thank Lorraine, my children, my mum and dad, Lorraine's mum and dad, Arsenal Football Club, the supporters, the FA, the press, and Steve and Mandy, me and Lorraine's sponsors, for all their support.

Went to GA in the evening with Lorraine. I was a very good meeting and enjoyed it. Went out and had a Chinese meal. It was beautiful. My first meal out of the clinic for six weeks. The people in the restaurant were brilliant to me and gave me great confidence.

SATURDAY 14 JANUARY
First day in the real world.

Weird feeling.

Had photographers around in the morning to take pictures of me, Lorraine, Charlie and Ben. They came in the house, took the pictures and then went left.

Went to watch the lads play Everton at Highbury which was great to be back at my second home. Sat in the directors' box and felt a bit gutted that the fans didn't sing my name, it's probably because no one knew I was there! But I do really worry about things like that, but Lorraine reassured me when she said, when we got home, the same that I was thinking. When I got home I was very tired. Rang a couple of the group to have a chat to see how they are. A couple of friends from NA rang to see how I was and that was good that they put themselves out to ring me. Still not sure when I can play again, but my priority is to stay on the programme and take a day at a time and if I stay clean and sober and not have a bet the football will follow. Had an 'Indian' and then watched football on TV and then went to bed.

SUNDAY 15 JANUARY

Took the kids swimming. I was a bit nervous about what people will say, but a couple of people came up to me and wished me all the best and that made me feel very happy. The press this morning was very good and there was some lovely pictures of Lorraine and the kids in the paper. There was just one silly article which was about Stan Bowles discussing the perils of gambling.

Sat in for the rest of the day, relaxed and looked forward to my first day's training.

MONDAY 16 JANUARY

First day training was brilliant. The lads were great, and so were all the staff. There were a lot of cameras there aimed at me – but it was just great to be back. It hadn't really sunk in how big news I have become over the last couple of days, and it was really good to read that the boss had said that he needs me back as soon as possible not just for Arsenal but also for the game and that made me feel great when I read it.

I rang Mr Friar to thank him for everything he had done and to tell him it is great to be back. There were also a couple of people who came up to me in the street and said good luck and all the best for the future, and that made me feel really good. So, thanks to those people.

Went to GA tonight and Lorraine went to GamAnon. I really enjoyed my GA meeting. I could really relate to a lot that was said and I also had some therapy. Lorraine said that she had enjoyed her meeting as well.

Lorraine cooked one of my favourite dinners tonight – chicken chasseur.

Unfortunately, it contains red wine, so she had to throw it away!

That's one of my favourite meals I cannot even contemplate having any more, but it was funny that she forgot that it had alcohol in it. It will be a while before she gets the hang of it. But she is brilliant and who cares about just one mistake from the best wife in the world!

TUESDAY 17 JANUARY
Received a lovely letter from someone at the FA to wish me all the best and who looks forward to seeing me in the England squad again as soon as possible. That made me feel very pleased.

Another good day at training, even though it was a very hard session. We did a lot of running when I trained with the youth team because the lads are playing Millwall tomorrow in the replay of the third round of the FA Cup. I wished I was playing tomorrow, but I'm not, so I've got to be patient and take a day at a time till the FA give me the go-ahead to play again. I've got to make sure I'm fit when I'm allowed to play again.

Went back down to the treatment centre tonight with Lorraine for counselling and for recovery. Met all the group again which was great. Lorraine enjoyed her meeting and it was brilliant. Long drive home, but it was worth it.

Thanks for coming down Lorraine, you'll never know how grateful I am, and also thanks again to Lorraine's mum for baby sitting because she's been a big help over the last seven weeks. Top mother-in-law!

WEDNESDAY 18 JANUARY
Didn't like what John Sadler had written in the *Sun* – Paul Merson is a mug not a martyr. When did I say I was a martyr, John?

Went shopping with Ben this morning at Watford and the people were brilliant. At least 10 people came up to me and said 'all the best Paul' and asked for my autograph, which makes me feel very good and gives me back my confidence.

Went with Lorraine to see my accountant, Steve, who has looked after all my finances brilliantly.

Went training at Highbury before the first team played. It was very hard; always is with Gary Lewin our physio.

After training I sat in the directors' box with Mr Friar who has been brilliant over the last seven weeks. The game was disappointing, the result even worse. A 2-0 defeat by Millwall.

Bought Charlie and Ben the Arsenal home kit tonight because Charlie's shirt is ruined and Ben hasn't had one before because he was too small.

I got their name and number 10 put on the back.

THURSDAY 19 JANUARY
Did a lot of hard work in training, and also had a little game which I got really so much out of. Most of all, to get properly fit, I need matches. Gary Lewin told me that they will know by tomorrow if I'm allowed to play friendlies behind closed doors and he is very confident I will be allowed and if I am that will be magic. I'll probably have two friendlies next week, fingers crossed.

Got my summons through today for my car accident which took place last August. Rang my solicitor and he said everything will be all right. I just hope I don't lose my licence because if I do it will be hard for me to get down to Southampton for recovery and counselling on Tuesday nights.

FRIDAY 20 JANUARY
Told by Arsenal that the FA will let me know on Monday if I will be able to play friendlies behind closed doors next week.

Watched Rugby League on TV and it brought back a lot of memories about gambling – 'bad move'.

Lorraine wasn't well and stayed in bed all day and I looked after the kids. I think it's all caught up with Lorraine from the last eight weeks.

SATURDAY 21 JANUARY
Went training this afternoon. Feel more like myself. Getting fitter and fitter every day.

Came home and watched the rugby on TV and I'm getting a

lot of the old feelings back about gambling, like one bet wouldn't hurt. But I didn't have a bet, and that's good.

Lorraine still isn't well but is getting better.

Talked to the rest of the group tonight and they are all all right and that's good.

SUNDAY 22 JANUARY
The worst day for eight weeks.

I really got the urge for a bet today and I also had a go at Lorraine and that was because I wanted a bet so desperately. I thought it would be all right just to have one bet but when I sat down and thought about it, I knew it was stupid.

Talked to Lorraine, her mum and dad, and then felt all right.

Took Charlie to Daniel's swimming party and had a good laugh. Came back and had a long chat on the phone to Steve and he said I was going to have those sort of days but I still didn't have a bet which is good.

GLAD I GOT THAT DAY OUT OF THE WAY.

MONDAY 23 JANUARY
Had my first drinks and drugs test today.

I felt very nervous when I was doing the test, but I don't know why because the last time I took cocaine was 13 November and the last drink I had was in France. When I got home I rang Steve Stephens and he said that my concerns were understandable because I might be thinking that it is still in my system since the last time I took drugs, but he said 'don't worry' and that made me feel so much better.

Training went very well and I'm working very hard.

Went to see my solicitor about my court appearance because I can't afford to lose my licence because of my recovery plan and the way my solicitor was talking I might keep it, fingers crossed.

Told that I can play friendly games which was great news and we've got a friendly on Wednesday against Peterborough and I'm looking forward to it.

WEDNESDAY 25 JANUARY
Played first match behind closed doors at our training ground but there was a few pressmen and a lot of photographers there. We played Peterborough and I played the whole 90 minutes and after the game I couldn't breathe. But I had played my first game and I was on my way back. The game went very well in the first half. It took that to get back in to the swing of things but in the second half I was very pleased with my passing and the main thing was that I enjoyed it. And we won 4-0.

THURSDAY 26 JANUARY
The day after the game I was very tired and stiff. It felt very much like a normal day and in the evening I went to my first AA meeting in St Albans. I felt very nervous when I first walked in but like the AA meetings in Southampton and everywhere else I've been, all the people in the room are the loveliest people you would like to meet anywhere. After the meeting I did the drying up and then went home.

WEDNESDAY 1 FEBRUARY
Got the phone call I had been waiting for for so long.

Gary Lewin rang me at about 10 o'clock to tell me that I'm allowed to play again and that I would be sub tonight against AC Milan.

The happiness I felt was unreal. The relief!!! And then the worry of how the fans are going to be.

Sky TV came round my house and asked if they could do an interview, but I said 'you will have to ask the FA and the club.' They did, they were given permission, so me and Lorraine did our first TV interview. I thought it came across very well.

Ten minutes before kick-off my counsellor Steve Stephens took me into the treatment room and asked me how I felt and said just go out and enjoy yourself. He told me that it wasn't many weeks ago that I would never have thought I would be playing tonight. He told me not to forget that making this comeback was nothing compared to what I had been through and what I am now doing with my life.

Sitting on the bench I couldn't wait to get on. The fans were brilliant. They sang my name all through the game. When I went on the reception I got from the fans made me feel so emotional.

I was very pleased at how I did and after the game one of the players came up to me and said it was great to see me back playing again after what I had been through. That made me feel very good.

THURSDAY 2 FEBRUARY

It was a great pleasure to read about myself in the papers – and that made a change. The reports on my comeback were brilliant.

Now it's up to me to keep the reports brilliant.

FRIDAY 3 FEBRUARY

AA meeting in Sheffield tonight prior to my first away game since leaving hospital. The club gave me permission to leave the team hotel to attend the meeting, which is good of them.

When me and Steve Stephens, my counsellor, went to the club to talk about what things I need to do, one of them was that I had to go to a meeting on a Friday night. The boss turned round and said how do we know he's going to go to the meeting and not go out for the night. I thought to myself that I would never do that. But I realized that I would have to work hard to get people to trust me again and that wouldn't come overnight.

Went to the meeting with my Arsenal track suit on and when I got in, I got a cup of tea and sat down next to some man and we started talking before the meeting. I asked him if this is a good meeting, and he said that he hadn't been to a bad meeting in nine years. I'll always remember what that man said that night.

SATURDAY 4 FEBRUARY

First away game at Sheffield Wednesday. My first full game for over four months. When we got off the coach at Sheffield there were a lot of people standing outside waiting for autographs and I thought a lot of kids wouldn't want mine, but everyone asked and I signed as many as I could. The manager said I'd probably play the first hour and see how it goes from there. Some of the crowd booed every time I got the ball but most of the home fans were very good. We lost 3-1 and ended up with nine men after Jack Adams and John Hartson were sent off. I played the whole game and felt absolutely knackered after the game. Couldn't wait to get to bed as soon as I got home – four months earlier I couldn't wait to get out when we got back from a match and have a drink.

SATURDAY 11 FEBRUARY

First goal since I've been back. Another day I'll never forget. My first full game at Highbury, the crowd were great. At first I was very nervous but when I started I couldn't have wished for a better game. In the second half Eddie Cool (McGoldrick) went down the wing and crossed it at the time I was just running into the box and the ball fell perfectly for me and I just hit it first time on the volley and it flew into the back of the net. The excitement was unreal. I've never had so much pleasure in scoring a goal in all my life. When I got back to the halfway line, I was nearly crying with joy and I couldn't run for about a minute after that. I nearly scored twice more but in the end they scored and we drew 1-1. But that still couldn't take the joy away from my goal. Home for a lovely Chinese take-away and watch TV.

TUESDAY 21 FEBRUARY

BOSS GETS THE SACK. What a bad day for me when I heard the news. It was one of the biggest setbacks since I've been out of treatment. The first thing that went through my mind was that the man who had stood by me so many times had gone and when the next manager comes in he might not like me and that he wouldn't understand my addictions and how I feel. Rang Steve Stephens and he had a long chat with me and said that if I had any problems about anything at the club talk to Mr Friar because Steve had asked Mr Friar to look after me, just like he has done all along.

Stewart (Houston) took over for the Forest game and we won 1-0, a great result. Went home straight after the game and felt much better. Yet, still cannot really believe the boss has been sacked. Going to miss him.

THANKS FOR EVERYTHING YOU HAVE DONE FOR ME AND LORRAINE, BOSS.

SUNDAY 5 MARCH

This was by far my worst game since I've been back in the team. (lost 1-0 to West Ham at Highbury). After the game it was very hard for me because before if I had a bad game I would have a lot to drink and get away from reality and forget about the game. But I couldn't and I had to go home and think about how I played and where I did well and most of all where I did badly. But looking back on it, it's better to go home and think about it, rather than get drunk. Well, that's my point of view. Watched a video and then went to bed.

THURSDAY 16 MARCH

What a night. We've just beaten Auxerre 1-0 away in the quarter-finals of the Cup Winners Cup, where no one gave us a chance. It was pretty hard for me after the game being in the dressing room with all the other lads on a high and then the directors brought loads of bottles of champagne in and the lads started to drink them to keep their high going. I found it very hard because I had to carry my high on without a drink. So I drank my orange and then got straight on the coach and sat as far away from the drinkers as I could. On the plane it was pretty hard again with all the lads drinking around me and the air stewardess asking if I want a beer. Of course, I said 'no' and asked for a diet Coke.

Thanks Gary Lewin and Wrighty. Gary for saying if you don't feel right come and sit with me because Gary is teetotal and

Wrighty because I sat next to him and he didn't have a drink because of that. I was well pleased for Stewart Houston because he's done a great job since the boss was sacked and he's been a great help to me for all the confidence he's given me and the way he's been with me.

SUNDAY 19 MARCH
Bad result losing 1-0 at Newcastle. But on the other hand I went into a bar for a soft drink for the first time since I've been out of treatment. I went in with Nigel (Winterburn) and Chris (Kiwomya). Naturally enough they were drinking their alcoholic drinks but I just drank diet Coke and felt very relaxed even though it was very packed. I was very pleased with myself. Actually, I rang Lorraine and said 'I'm just stopping to have a drink with Nigel and Chris'. I could tell by Lorraine's voice that she thought for one second that I was 'drinking'. But when I told her I wasn't, she was all right, and said 'have a good time'.

MONDAY 20 MARCH
It's my birthday today. I'm feeling really tired. Went to Brent Cross shopping centre, with Lorraine and new baby son Sam, to buy some clothes with my birthday money.

FRIDAY 24 MARCH
The worst day since I've been out of treatment.
   Went training this morning and was feeling very tired and depressed. I felt bad. I felt frightened because I've felt really good since I've been out but today was different. I asked to see our physio Gary Lewin and he took me into a little room where we normally get weighed. Gary asked me what was wrong and I just broke down in tears and said it's getting hard. Gary was brilliant about it and listened to my problems. I confided to him that I was getting feelings of guilt because Lorraine was getting up with Sam all the time. Lorraine wasn't complaining, in fact she was great, she didn't say anything but I still felt terribly guilty about

it. I rang Lorraine to ask her if she wanted to go away for the weekend but she said she would love to but didn't want to leave the kids with my mum and dad because Sam gets up two or three times a night and it wasn't fair.

When I got home I talked to Lorraine and then discussed it with my sponsor, Steve, who had become such a good friend, and a much needed one at this critical time, to tell him how I had been feeling. I started crying again. Steve, who had suffered these problems himself, explained that it was not unusual to feel like this. He was grateful that I had rung him. He told me I had done well to contact him, because I felt like a bet and a drink just so that I could get out of this state for the day. I didn't like being depressed because I remembered what had happened when a friend I had met in treatment put a knife in himself because he felt the way I was feeling. My sponsor suggested that I rang Steve Stephens, my counsellor, but I said he was away on holiday, but two minutes after putting down the phone to Steve, my counsellor rang and we had a long chat. He made me feel great. He said precisely what Steve had already told me, but he also said that your worst day today is better than your best day when you were betting, drinking and using cocaine. And that's true. And it made me feel so much better. A lot of the way I was feeling was down to not attending my meetings for one reason or another, such as training, matches and the best one of all just feeling tired and saying to myself 'well, I don't feel like a drink, so I won't go tonight.' But, they are not wrong when they say that alcohol is cunning and baffling and creeps up at you when you least expect it.

Went to GA and 'shared' about my week, and there were a lot of tears. But the people in the room understood because they've been there themselves before and they're understanding. I felt brilliant when I came out.

I've learned today that I have got to keep on attending my meetings and I must never ever get complacent.

I'm going to bed now, I'm so pleased this day is over. Even though it was a bad one, I learned a real lot today and it's made me feel even stronger. Thanks Lorraine for being here for me and thanks mum and dad for dropping everything and coming over for the weekend to help me and Lorraine.

SATURDAY 25 MARCH

Woke at about 9.40. Lorraine let me lay in because I've been feeling tired, especially after that bad day yesterday.

Went to the park to watch my eldest boy Charlie play football for an hour and a half which he loves doing – definitely takes after his dad! Came back and watched TV in between playing in the garden with the kids on a bouncy castle which I hired for the day and which is such great fun for the kids. I've never had so many Saturdays off, and because I have stopped my addictions and no longer bet, drink or use drugs, I've got loads of time for the kids, plenty of time for playing in the garden like today. Six months ago I would have been glued to the TV full time watching racing and not really worrying about anything else.

Went out for a meal with Neil and Elaine, who we used to go out with all the time but we hadn't been socializing with since I came out of treatment. It doesn't matter how much I tell Neil about my addictions, he doesn't understand because tonight, at the table, I was telling him about my problems yesterday and then he said 'don't you think you're putting yourself under too much pressure stopping all your addictions at once, why don't you give one up at a time over a distance of time.' Me and Lorraine burst out laughing at the table. We knew that I've tried stopping one or the other before, but it never worked, and that's why I can't get involved in any addictions at any time, ever.

SUNDAY 26 MARCH

Mothers' Day. Got up early because Lorraine had booked me a sun bed at the health club so I had to get up and go and not sit around. But when I woke up I felt great, I felt as though I was back on the programme and happy again. Played football in the garden with the boys and then tidied up the study. After a lovely dinner, I also tidied up the kitchen for Lorraine and then bathed the kids and put them to bed around 6.30, which is the time they usually go to bed, like good little boys. Mum and dad have gone home but they have been brilliant again over the weekend and I can't thank them enough.

Spoke to one of the group this afternoon and she's doing great. She said she didn't think Jackie is drinking but she's switched herself off from the rest of us, but at least she hasn't picked up a drink and that's made me feel better. That news ended my weekend on a high note.

Hang in there, Jackie.

MONDAY 27 MARCH

Back at training today and a few of the lads are asking questions about Friday. But I just said I had to go somewhere because something was wrong.

Went to GA tonight and Lorraine went to GamAnon. I was pleased that Lorraine went because she needs to go to her meetings. Because of the birth of our baby Sam she hasn't been able to go. The meeting was good tonight. I 'shared' for about 15 minutes about how I had been over the past week and what my gambling was like when I was betting every minute of the day. I would sometimes go into a betting shop and instead of having a double or treble, I would have a ten horse accumulator and try and win thousands in just one hit.

I'm going to bed much happier now because I've had a long chat with my sponsor Steve about my meetings I had been to today, and the fact that there isn't a midweek game so that I can do all my meetings and I feel great because I'm back on the programme.

DO YOUR MEETINGS.

TUESDAY 28 MARCH

An up and down day.

Woke feeling great, took the kids to school and then went to the health club for a steam and sauna. The club had given me the day off so I can go for treatment. Left at 11.30, said 'bye' to Lorraine who I thought was fine. Met my counsellor Steve

Stephens at the service station near the treatment centre because he's off on a two week holiday. We talked for nearly two hours in the Wimpy about how I feel and everything that's going on in my life and he makes me feel great. We talked about last Friday and what made me feel like that and he said I am going go get those sort of days but I must just stick in there just like I did at the training ground on Friday. Left Steve feeling absolutely great and headed for the tennis club to meet with Joan, the doctor's wife, and a couple of friends who I played tennis when I was in treatment. It's the first time I've seen them since I left and it was marvellous to see them because when I was in treatment I used to love playing tennis because it broke up the hard days and I could take everything out on the tennis balls when I was feeling angry, tired, or lonely. Played two sets. Me and my partner lost the first set 7-6 and then won the next 6-4. Joan and her partner might beat us one day but don't hold your breath!

After dinner headed off to the place I owe everything to, my treatment centre. It was great to see Jackie back again after being away for two weeks but she hasn't had a drink, she just isolated herself but it's great to have her back.

From the treatment centre, I rang Lorraine.

She was in tears.

Lorraine told me that everything had suddenly got on top of her, and she felt terribly depressed.

I felt guilty and sad because she was there for me on Friday when I was bad, but now she needs me and I am 90 miles away having a meeting.

When I put the phone down, really bad things went through my mind, such as she's going to leave me. Everything had caught up with her and she doesn't want to be with me any more because of the person I used to be, and that I'm a bad husband when I thought I was doing really well. But that's the way I was feeling and that how alcoholics and addicts and compulsive gamblers think.

I rang Lorraine's sponsor, Mandy, and asked her to phone her. Went to my meeting and 'shared' about how Lorraine was and how if affected me. They were very understanding because a lot of them had been through it with their partners and they said that I have got to realize that Lorraine lives with the disease and that she has been through such a lot. They did help me but it was a massive shock that Lorraine broke down because she was so strong all through the last five to six months and it shook me.

Drove back from Southampton and had a long chat with Lorraine about how she feels and where we are going from here. There were a lot of tears. But we went to bed much happier and closer together. Mandy, Lorraine's sponsor, rang back at about 11.30 to see how we were, and that shows what a great friend she is.

HANG IN THERE LORRAINE, I LOVE YOU AND I WILL ALWAYS BE THERE FOR YOU LIKE YOU WERE FOR ME.

WEDNESDAY 29 MARCH
A good day. Lorraine feels much better and that's brilliant. I did all the housework to give her a rest, which makes me feel good because when I was drinking I could never find time to do things like that.

Watched England play Uruguay at Wembley tonight on TV and the dreams are still there. Watching that game, made me want it even more, wanting, that is, to play for England again.

THURSDAY 30 MARCH
This has been a really good day.

Training went very well, the team spirit is really good and everyone's very relaxed even though we've got two big games coming up that we have to win.

Home from work and Lorraine said my mate from treatment is coming for dinner so I cooked a spaghetti, which is about the only thing I can cook. Took Lorraine to the shops to get the ingredients for dinner. If anyone is wondering why I'm putting all this in my diary, they ought to try to understand that routine, normal things like this are big things for me. It's normality.

My mate came down and we had a long chat about what it

was like for me in treatment, and the things we went through. It brought back some good and some bad times but I got a lot out of our talk. Before my mate left we made a pact to ring each other once a week. We went to an AA meeting together that night and it was great to see him looking so good.

SATURDAY 1 APRIL

Another great day as we beat Norwich 5-1 and I scored. Great. I hadn't scored for a few games so that was wonderful. I put that down to getting back on my programme and doing my meetings this week. Went round to my sponsor's house with Lorraine and Sam, because Charlie and Ben were staying at my mum and dad's house. Over our usual Chinese take-away we had yet another long chat. Sorry, but we kept them up until 1.30 a.m. when we finally left because we had to feed Sam. I drove. Brilliant. Lorraine would always have to drive me home at that time of night but now that I don't drink I can drive her and Sam home. It's little things like that that make me feel great.

SUNDAY 2 APRIL

Went to watch my two younger brothers play football. Sunday dinner at my mum and dad's, came home in time to watch the Coca-Cola Cup Final between Liverpool and Bolton on TV. It brought back a lot of happy memories because two years ago I scored one and made the winner and got the Man of the Match award. I'm very proud of that because it is one of the special memories I have so far in my football career. It's been a great weekend.

MONDAY 3 APRIL

Day off, so went to 'Toys 'R' Us' to get Ben his birthday presents in time for the big day on the fifteenth.

George Graham rang this evening to have a chat and to return my phone call last Friday. He's doing well, he tells me, and that's good news. We chatted for a while and I still call him 'boss' because of the respect I have for the man. He told me to keep in

Drinking with George Graham, Perry Groves and David O'Leary, 1989.

'Doing the Merson', the gesture
that now makes me cringe.
(Photograph: Daily Mirror)

Even worse, Charlie 'doing a Merson'.
(Photograph: Loaded Magazine)

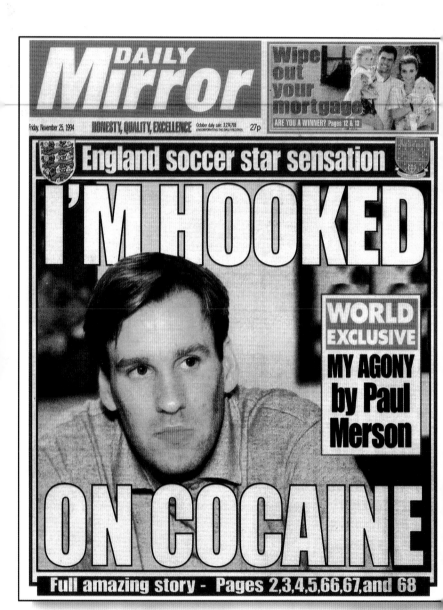

The front page that said it all.

The bad old days.

Giving Charlie his birthday cake on 18 December 1994, my first day release from Marchwood Priory Hospital.

Pages from my life story which I had to write and then read out to my therapy group as part of my treatment.

The Pre-School Years (1-5 years)

① I was born on the 20th March 1968 in park royal hopsital Harsleden, North West London. I'm the oldest of 4 Children which is one sister and two other brothers who from this day get on really well together. My mum is 9 years younger than my dad, my mum was a housewife and had partime jobs when she could get them, but usly she would work from home, and my dad is a coalman and as been for the hole of is life. My mum and dad where quite poor we lived on the top floor of a house which was small

(5-12 years of age)

down the park . . .

. . . always say don't I was becoming a sad boy this was because I was wetting the bed, always coming home from school asking my dad if he was staying intonigh cause he would always go out and play cards alnight and my mum would some-time get me to ring up my dad at the card school to see when he was coming home but the man on the phone would say he was not hear but I could hear is voice say tell him I'm not hear and I would be crying my eyes out, and I would still be crying in bed. And somtimes my dad would hide me in my mums bedroom to see whene she hed her nages and then he would nick them and go and gamble it away.

Monday
16–349   Week 3
Martin Luther King, Jr. Day   Holiday (USA)
○ Full Moon

16

First days training was brilliant the lads where great, and so where all the staff they where a book of camras there to take photos of me and it was great to be back, but it hasn't really sunk in how big news I have become over the last couple of days and it was really good to read that the boss had said that he state needs me back as soon as possible not just for arsenal but also for the game and that made me feel great when I read it. I went to see my agents jeff + jerome today just to thank them for what they have done over the last 6 weeks I also rang mr fraw today to thank him for everything he has done and to tell him it is great to be back. There was also a couple of people who come up to me when I was walking to jeff + jerome and said good luck and all the best for the future and that make me feel really good so thank you to them people. Went to G A tonight and lorraine went pamleon I really enjoyed my G A meeting, I could really reate realte to a lot that was said and I also gave som trapy and lorraine said she enjoyed her meeting as well. Lorraine cooked one of my favriote dinners tonight which is chicken which as red wine in so she had to throw it away so that one dinner I can not have anymore but it was funny that she forgot that it had red wine in it cos it will take a while before she gets the hang of it but she is brilliant and whats one mistake from the best wife in the world.

Pages from the daily diary I had to keep as part of my therapy. The changes in the handwriting perhaps reflect the turmoil I was going through.

Wednesday tuesday
340–25   Week 49

6

Todays been a really hard day I have had my morning interview and gave me a other thing today was frightened me to drugs after I filled and told her that I was know that I was both shocked but of or a few think about it your word are a to drink soon as I had had went out or the last place drunk on gambling, drunk and ready by monday morning, after dinner I asked the to peel my apple but she I went to the aftercare meeting took the apple and after the meeting I all the other people who have been for and after the meeting I have to have a drink to enjoy yourself.

with the police and they were very understanding which I was very pleased with. the that I was told I was a acholic and addicted out the asser on Saturday. this both of these. I rang lorraine of these and she seemed very seconds she said if you acholic cause the way I used one dinner I couldn't stop and if I ever I would not come home till I was drunk had closed. I was given Step I today drugs and I have to have it I had dinner tonight and after dinner I lady for a sharp knife to peel I was not allowed and she peeled it in the kicthen. I in the evening where in treatment come back relised that you don't

Return of the joker

PAUL MERSON forgot his tears yesterday as he shared a laugh and joke with some important mates.

The Arsenal star returned to training for the first time since his football career was shattered by revelations of addiction to drugs, drink and gambling.

And a slimline Merson was back with orders from manager George Graham—no special treatment.

"Nothing has changed, everyone is looked after the same here," said Graham. "It doesn't matter who you are—whether it's Paul, Ian Wright or

Tears of last week forgotten as Merson rejoins his mates in

LONDON & SOUTH
SCORE!

YOUR LOCAL *Daily Mirror* ALL-ACTION PULLOUT

WELL DONE MER-SON: Arsenal's Paul Merson salutes the crowd after the goal that helped the crisis-torn club to victory over Palace. Eddie McGoldrick joins in the celebrations.
Picture: JASON SHILLINGFORD

Paul's Mer-gic!

WELCOME to week one of Mirror Sport's new Score, the brightest soccer pullout of them all. The big names, the big games, the big action in YOUR area. It's all here in the No 1 soccer pullout.

INSIDE KLIN FOILED
PAGE 8

YOUR WOLFING IT UP!
PAGE 5

SUPER SCORE! FREE £1 BET
Ladbrokes
PAGE 12

Now Paul's ready for a starring role again

MICHAEL HART on the chances of Arsenal's prodigal son returning, full-time, to

BREATHLESS: Merson feels the pace during his return . IT'S thirsty work for Paul after a full game Pic: DALE CHERRY

P AUL MERSON, having overcome the first hurdle in his comeback programme, could now be in Arsenal's starting line-up for Saturday's visit to Sheffield Wednesday.

Arsenal manager George Graham will

Welcome back Mer-Son

By MARK IRWIN

A RSENAL bad boy Paul Merson yesterday ended ten weeks of hell and declared: "It's

Eddie McGoldrick, Ian Selley, Paul Dickov and Jimmy Carter, he made his mark with a series of telling passes from midfield.

But all those weeks away eventually took their toll. And by the end he was clutching his sides in agony and gasping for breath.

"I thought it went well," he said, "but I must admit I was very red in the last five minutes."

Arsenal have been ordered to pay £1,750 to Swansea. And if he makes of he makes ances.

IT'S MUDDY GREAT TO BE BACK!

By MARTIN SAMUEL

MUDDIED, if not unbowed, Paul Merson began his footballing rehabilitation in a tiny, rain-sodden corner of Hertfordshire at 11am yesterday.

The bright lights, the highlights that sucked him into a world cursed by drink and gambling, must have seemed a million miles away.

As the final whistle blew he collapsed, doubled up, after trudging through 90 minutes against a hastily pulled-together side from Second Division Peterborough.

Yet when Merson emerged an hour later, looking smart in casual faded yellow trousers and a black leather jacket, there was a bounce in his step that said it all.

He posed briefly for pictures, admitting "It's great to be back"

in between — the flick he

Merson zinging in rain

GET STUCK IN . . Merson is so determin

MAN ON THE RUN: Paul Merson yesterday

Paul's return is like signing a new player

Crystal Palace 0 Arsenal 3

STEWART HOUSTON compared him to Roy of The Rovers. But Paul Merson does not go into pubs these days.

He has returned, though. And he is busy rebuilding a career many felt was finished when he checked into of Highbury and into rehab just before Christmas

Rehabilitated, rejuvenated, reborn. Merson has mastered three R's. And he used them to incredible effect when given a chance in the suspended

Without John Harston, Arsenal wielded Chris Kiwomya with Merson in a free role behind.

It was Houston's idea and it was a masterstroke. Suddenly, Arsenal had the old Paul Merson back. The young Paul Merson; Merson who won Not Merse who won

This was the alcoholic. the championship at the age of 21 playing as a striker.

It is a long time since we have seen him. Yet he was present at Selhurst Park, scoring one goal, always threatening, often unstoppable. the man Palace could not control.

Arsenal have scored four goals under Houston and Merson. The new manager has them all rehabilitated, and the hand in hand with ballet, something to prove. Hollywood would love it.

two further versatile tale

The first placed at Kiwomya w their secret on which run which second and had compensati has had too. But emerged he So beat only alr but int money

And turn may 1 above h

Had been have and not gone but

Flexible

Houston said: "Paul been like a new sign Arsenal. People for

Merson: Misery is all behind me now

PAUL MERSON vowed not to return to his bad-boy ways after making his Arsenal comeback against AC Milan.

The England star, playing for the first time since his cocaine, drink and gambling revelations, admitted: "Now I've got to repay everybody — with goals. And there's no way I'm going to get complacent and slip back to old ways. I feel the best I've ever done and I want to stay that way."

Merson, a late substitute, added: "It was brilliant to be back and I owe so much to so many people. Some people might have said 'well he's brought it all on himself', but hopefully they realise I've got a disease which won't just go away. The fans proved what I had already believed — that they are the best there is . . . brilliant. I could easily have cried a few tears out there."

Look who's back

AFTER being Anonymous Paul among fellow addicts, nothing could have felt better than hearing the words: "Merse, over here, Merse," screamed across a training field by a team-mate.

This was England soccer star Paul Merson back training with Arsenal yesterday after six weeks' absence to sort out his drink, drugs and gambling problems.

● Full story: P50

Back at last, the new me.

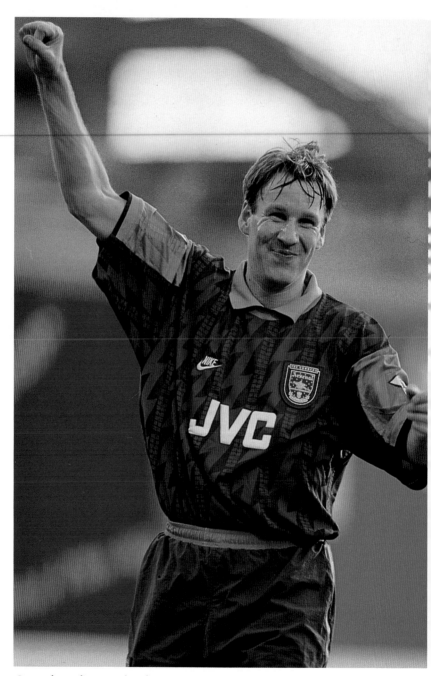

One of my first goals after my return, against Crystal Palace on
25 February. *(Photograph: Clive Brunskill, Allsport)*

touch and if there was ever any problem just to ring him. That was great to hear. It was very weird talking to him as a friend and not as my boss any more.

Went to GA. Just listened and it was another good meeting.

TUESDAY 4 APRIL

Another good day, apart, that is, for the little crash I had in the car! I hit a parked car when I was parking and ended up doing more damage to my car. I was gutted but that was a good reaction because if it had happened six months ago I would have been more interested in having a bet or going to the pub or not really caring because I had other things on my mind.

Took part in an FA drugs campaign with England coach Terry Venables. Went very well. I spoke about drugs and told everyone that I had been to hell and back. I explained just how hard it had been in treatment. When I was telling everyone, I felt good because I'm getting more confident about myself now. I tried to get it across that if you don't have that first drink you will not get drunk and if you don't have that first drug you'll be all right and you won't want to get high or addicted. I hope the kids will listen because it's not worth it – you can throw everything away and to play football for a living has got to be the best job in the world. I've been given a second chance and I'm going to give it my best shot – a day at a time.

THANKS TO EVERYONE WHO HAS STUCK BY ME.

8

ONE DAY AT A TIME

My first day of freedom from the FA-approved Marchwood Priory Hospital turned out to be a day of great emotion for me, but the greatest feeling was sheer relief to be out.

The biggest ordeal was the news conference at a hotel near the FA's headquarters at Lancaster Gate, the white-walled Park Court. I picked up a smart double-breasted pinstripe suit and red tie at a neighbour's because I couldn't risk going back home as there were so many journalists waiting to pounce. A dozen TV cameras, arc lights, and every newspaper represented, some with more than one journalist – it was an intimidating atmosphere after all I'd been through.

It took less than a minute – just the third question – before I broke down in tears.

Initially I was composed. 'This has been the hardest six weeks of my life. It has changed me completely. I am starting to grow up now,' I said. But I wept uncontrollably when I was asked to describe a typical day's therapy at the rehabilitation centre. I slowly bowed my head and began crying. It was a harmless enough question – on the surface. But the enormity of what I had been going through suddenly hit me.

George Graham put a protective arm around me, and then he rested his hand on my knee and told me to leave it to him. At that point I was incapable of answering any more questions. The tears were no put-up job for the cameras. No one could stage-manage that! All the hurt and pain of letting down my family, my friends, my football club and the supporters, but most of all the harm I had done to myself, all came gushing out.

When I had regained my composure I explained, 'I thought I would be all right today but there's been a lot of tears in there and this is the most difficult thing I've done in my life... I am an alcoholic. I can never take another drink. It is hard to explain but alcoholics will understand. I can't start preaching – I've messed my life about as it is. I've got a choice in life. I either go back to the booze and the gambling, or I go the other way. It is not out of the question, I believe, for me to get back into the Arsenal team, and then all the way to the England team.'

My six weeks of treatment had given back some meaning to my life. I watched football – it was good to watch it, to appreciate what I was missing. You get into a lifestyle of playing football every week. Suddenly it had been taken away from me and I appreciate now how much I missed it. The game of football still means so much to me – to be playing the best sport in the world.

I was glad when the press conference was over, but at the same time I had been happy to talk about my problems. It had been part of my therapy to talk openly, and I began to discover that I was able to tell people frankly about what had been happening to me.

There was a joint statement from the FA, Arsenal and the PFA: 'He is under no illusions that if he returns to his old ways, disciplinary action of the severest kind will be taken against him. Over the next few weeks, he will be free to mix with family, friends and workmates. It will be a testing time for him. The FA has received medical advice that his rehabilitation appears to have been a success so far, but still has a significant way to go. We've also been informed that a point will be reached when to delay his return to competitive football would be detrimental to his progress. That point has not been reached at this moment. But if his progress is maintained, it is anticipated a decision will be taken early in February as to when he may be able to resume his career.'

Sky TV screened it live, and I rang Lorraine and told her to watch it. She was shocked.

From then on my life revolved around attending Alcoholics Anonymous, Gamblers Anonymous, Narcotics Anonymous, and therapy sessions back at Marchwood. Life was to be lived under the AA maxim: 'One day at a time.'

My first move as a 'free man' was to attend a two-hour session of Gamblers Anonymous. No more would my social life hinge on a night out in the pub. I was made fully aware of the consequences of failing to attend therapy.

If I do not go and get the medicine I will not get any better. Therapy, football and my family fill my life totally. There is no room for anything else. And that is my present and my future.

The first step back was my comeback with Arsenal, together with constant therapy. I trained at Marchwood Priory, running in the grounds and working out in the gym. My motivation was the day I would make my return to the pitch. I kept in trim during the rehabilitation period of six weeks, although I didn't kick a ball until the last week, when some of the training staff came down from Arsenal, and my weight remained the same – I'm pleased with that. Even so, I was well aware that you can train every day of the week, but until you play in a match your fitness is never properly put to the test.

It was so vital to me to play again that the FA knew that too long a delay would risk affecting my recovery programme. I was still very much in a vulnerable state. I was back training with my team-mates at London Colney for the first time on 17 January. The club were determined to keep my return to training as normal and as low-key as possible. It was 9.45 a.m. when I passed through the gates of the training ground, a short drive from my home, to be welcomed back by all my old pals.

A brief kick-about behind the changing rooms was followed by light jogging round the pitch with the rest of the first-team squad and a series of sprints under the watchful eye of assistant manager Stewart Houston. A few minutes of reflex work followed before I broke off with Ray Parlour, John Jensen, Martin Keown, Nigel Winterburn, Mark Flatts and Highbury new boy John Hartson for a game of two-touch, organized for the benefit of waiting photographers. Then, while George Graham worked with his first-team squad through set-piece routines for the FA Cup replay with Millwall, I went for a forty-five-minute match with the reserves.

We all had a great laugh, and it was like nothing had changed. But one very important thing had changed. Me. It might have seemed as though I'd never been away. But I had. And the boys found out that the old Merson no longer existed. There would be no more drinking sessions for me. I think they were shocked.

I was encouraged that I lasted the whole session. The smile was well and truly back on my face that day.

Although it was good to be back, I knew there was plenty of hard work to be done in private, away from the gaze of the publicity machine. I had missed the jokes and the camaraderie of team training, and needed to get back into a normal routine. Everyone gets treated the same – it doesn't matter who you are. Because I had lost a bit of weight and looked quite slim, it didn't mean I was fit.

The next step was a match. Any match.

Date: 26 January. Venue: London Colney. Time: 11 a.m. On a rain-sodden pitch I made my comeback in a match specially arranged to give me a game. It was private apart from the usual crowd of journalists and photographers. The FA had given the OK for me to play after I passed a routine drugs test.

I returned in weather more suited to building arks than placing free-kicks. Not so much back with a bang as a squelch. Just ten minutes into the second half I had my hands on my knees. I was knackered. Even so, I managed the odd flick here, the neat turn there. We were three up in thirty minutes – although I must admit it had nothing to do with any of my efforts! But I did set up the fourth goal for Jimmy Carter late on, at a time when exhaustion was getting the better of me.

When the final whistle blew I collapsed in a heap, doubled up, after trudging through ninety minutes against a hastily pulled together side from Second Division Peterborough. My first full game in ten weeks. It had been great to be back in an Arsenal shirt. I thought it went well, although it was a bit of a struggle in the last few minutes. But it was just the start.

An hour later, after I had showered and changed, I posed briefly for pictures and give an interview to all the reporters.

Five days later the club wanted me to appear in a friendly, again at Peterborough. It was to be a competitive game, and for that the club needed FA approval. George Graham contacted Graham Kelly at the FA, but because it was to be played before the public they refused permission for me to appear.

The boss pencilled in the game against the European champions AC Milan in the Super Cup for my first-team return. At first I thought they wanted me to play in the away leg, away from the media hype, but everyone realized there would be a media circus no matter where I played. The boss decided he wanted to put me on the bench for the first leg at Highbury on 1 February, but first the FA had to give their permission and left it until the very morning of the match. That day was the first possible date that I could make a return in a competitive game in public.

The club originally asked for permission to play me in the second leg of the Super Cup and that was given. But I had to wait until the morning of the game before it was decided I could play at Highbury.

I was ready. I had pushed myself through a punishing daily routine of 500 sit-ups. I felt as fit as I had ever done in my entire career. Because of the work I had done, my stamina was better than when I had my enforced lay-off. I used to be knackered after training and tired in matches, but I felt stronger and fitter. Even so, I still needed time to integrate back into the game.

My touch was still there, and all I wanted was for the crowd to be patient with me. I'd heard some people say you lose your touch when you are out for so long, but that had not happened to me. I feel my touch is still there and I have been working hard to improve my stamina, which was perhaps a bit suspect before. I can say it's better than ever. The sit-ups programme had increased my abdominal strength enormously. That is where the stamina to last games comes from. I had shed 10lb over the past few weeks and that had been replaced by muscle. People said I looked leaner, and fitter.

Once again George Graham was great, making public statements to the effect that my muscle tone was better than it had been for about two years. I'd lost nearly a stone, and I felt confident that I would be all right with all the muscle I'd built up. There was constant talk about new signings but I felt like I was a new signing for the club. I'd been away a long time and had come back a completely different person. It was again up to me – no one else.

The big comeback brought more tears. It seems I'm worse than Gazza! But by the end there was a huge smile from yours truly. I was back at last. I loved it, and just as important to me, so did the fans. I must admit I was very nervous about facing them again. I didn't know what I would have done if I had come out and they were booing and jeering. I wouldn't have been able to come to terms with losing their goodwill and support, because that was so important to me. If I had got a bad reception I would have tried to win them over with my football, but it wouldn't have been easy.

In the event the 38,000 capacity crowd was full of sympathy for me. The fans were almost as emotional as me. They chanted my name from the moment it was announced to the crowd that I was on the substitutes' bench. They were almost begging George Graham to bring me on. When he sent me on in the number fourteen shirt, there was a huge roar. A spontaneous chant of 'There's only one Paul Merson' echoed around that famous stadium. The fans welcomed me back and I cannot thank them enough.

Just sixteen minutes – that's all I got. But I lapped up every second. It was only natural that I felt a little nervous. It was like making my debut all over again. It was just brilliant to be back.

My first touch of the ball was greeted with a sliding tackle from the unsympathetic but efficient Paolo Maldini. But gradually I eased my way back into the big time. I thoroughly enjoyed side-stepping Marcel Desailly and sweeping a typical pass with the outside of the boot to the feet of full-back Nigel Winterburn. That was really satisfying.

But after a few sprints I was puffing a bit, my hands on my hips again. I was still in urgent need of match-fitness.

When the Dutch referee signalled the end of a goalless draw I savoured the applause of the fans and as a mark of appreciation applauded back, turning to all four sides of the stadium. It was my way of saying a huge thank you to the fans. A picture was taken of me with the word 'Hope' up on the electronic score-board. Nothing could have been more appropriate. Hope was the key to recovery.

Every day is a fresh challenge. I wake up each morning ready to fight another day against all my addictions. I believe I can do it. I'm making a big effort. I have a new perception of life and how wrong my life had been going.

It all began with drink and gambling. The evils of alcohol. In the past I would laugh whenever I heard anyone say something like that. I thought boozing it up made me somebody, one of the lads. Now I know different. It has been a painful journey to the realization of what I was doing to myself.

Drink and gambling drove me to the verge of insanity. Now on Mondays I attend Gamblers Anonymous in Wembley, and on Friday evenings it's GA at Barnet. In between I go to meetings with Alcoholics Anonymous and Narcotics Anonymous. I attend AA meetings every Wednesday or Thursday at St Albans, near my home, and I also travel to my group sessions at the Marchwood Hospital. It's a pretty full schedule. Normally the group sessions begin at 8 p.m. and finish around 10.30.

I have come to appreciate other people's problems as well as my own. Listening to members of the group, as they open up their very souls, makes you think. What we call a 'shared' experience can be very moving, and sometimes you relate to others very closely. That happened to me in my second GA meeting. I went there only once before I confessed, and then went back on the very first night of my release from Marchwood Priory.

It was the most eerie feeling of my life. A member of the group got up and said the usual opening: 'I'm —. I'm a compulsive gambler . . . ' He went on to explain how he had been a compulsive gambler for twenty-one years. Immediately I thought to myself, this guy has been coming here for twenty-one years and this is just my second meeting. Fucking hell, am I going to be coming here for the next twenty-one years? Others then 'shared' – one had been coming to GA for eighteen years – and so it went on. I thought I'd still be going to GA when I was fifty.

Now I hope I am.

I came out of those meetings feeling good. It was always an uplifting experience to listen to others trying hard to overcome their problems and succeeding, and of course for me to have the chance to unburden myself.

GA taught me the first rule of overcoming addiction – first to accept your problem and then to admit to it openly. It seems simple enough, but in reality it's the hardest part. For years I could never see myself as addicted to anything, let alone admit it to anyone.

That first meeting at GA alone has been of enormous help to me. They told me I must take it day by day, hour by hour, even minute by minute. It was so helpful to me seeing people in the same position. There are all kinds there – successful businessmen and quite ordinary people – and I would never have realized the extent of the problem and truly thought I was alone. Lorraine also attends meetings with another group, specifically for partners and relatives of compulsive gamblers, and says she can understand the problem and how to tackle it.

I tried to keep my problems away from football, or at least that was my intention. I knew that betting on football matches that I was involved in would land me deep in hot water with the FA. But I never placed a bet on games that I had any influence over or was involved in, although I've bet on virtually everything else. But now my gambling has come to an end. I hope my experience will serve as a warning to others. Perhaps the best warning I can give is to stress just how tough it's been to stop gambling.

The day I first 'shared' my experiences in my GA group, on

a Monday evening at Wembley, I was shaking and there was such a massive lump in my throat that I could hardly talk. Yet I should have been used to group therapy by now, after my time at Marchwood Priory and attending therapy groups on a regular basis. This was different, though. This was the night I had to open up entirely about myself all over again to my new group: 'I am Paul, I am a compulsive gambler…'

But now I am able to talk much more freely about my innermost thoughts because I have come to trust the people in my group and, in fact, come to rely on them. There is nothing special that I talk about; just how my week has gone, how I am feeling, how I am coping, if I'm experiencing any bad times. Basically you have to be open and honest. Anything you say that isn't is quickly spotted by other members of the group and they let you know. At the Monday group at Wembley you have to get up from your chair and walk over to a chair at the head of the group to talk. On Friday's session at Barnet, you have comfortable seating and don't need to move chairs, and you even get tea and a piece of cake at half-time. I always come out of these meetings, whether I've spoken to the group or listened to others, feeling on a high.

Whenever I have a Thursday free I go back to Marchwood to see the group and sit in on the sessions. Groups at Narcotics Anonymous are not that big, sometimes as few as eight people, although there can be between fifteen and twenty. In NA everyone takes their turn to talk. All of our group have become very close and one guy travelled from his home in Bournemouth to see my first four comeback games. That illustrates the strength of the fellowship that exists within the group. I talk to him on the phone about twice a week. Full credit to him – he has gone eighteen months without having 'picked up' – used drugs again.

In NA I have heard the most harrowing life stories. One of my group used to inject himself with heroin. When he ran out of it, he would inject himself with vodka and gin, straight into his veins to get himself drunk as fast as possible. Frightening!

Drug addicts tend to be a lot younger than alcoholics and those who attend GA. One young heroin addict neglected his meetings, and then opted out, but ended up coming back a year later – after stabbing himself in the chest. That scared the shit out of me too.

That guy was lucky to survive. He tried to kill himself, and that's a haunting image that has tucked itself into my mind.

I get those days of deep depression that everyone is prone to after coming off one addiction, but I've had to come off three. I had a really dark day when I had not been long back at training with my team-mates after being released from my intensive therapy at Marchwood. But when I had that bad day, when I collapsed with fear, the first thing that sprang into my head was that heroin addict and how he tried to stab himself to death. Powerful feelings came over me. I had flashbacks to all those times I was drunk and in the gutter. I know that if I ever relapsed, failed to go to my meetings, went back to my addictions, I'd end up trying to commit suicide by stabbing myself.

One guy 'shared' his story and told us that he used to consider people in his company who didn't drink, gamble, smoke or take drugs were the biggest bores alive. That's precisely how I used to think. I didn't have a clue what people lived for if they didn't drink, gamble and take drugs. How do they get by in life? How do they enjoy themselves? I used to wonder.

Of course there is no cure for addiction, but my group meetings are such an important part of my life now. AA differs from GA in that you are not obliged to talk to the group if you don't want to, although you become a lot stronger when you do face them. At the end of every AA meeting we all make a circle, hold hands and we all repeat the serenity prayer:

'GOD GRANT ME THE SERENITY TO ACCEPT THE THINGS I CANNOT CHANGE, THE COURAGE TO CHANGE THE THINGS I CAN, AND THE WISDOM TO KNOW THE DIFFERENCE. KEEP COMING BACK. IT WORKS IF YOU WORK AT IT.'

I say it over and over again during the day. It means that I cannot change things the way they are, but, with courage, I can change the things that are in my power to change. In other words I have the power to stop doing the things that do me harm.

The last phrase of the serenity prayer is not said at GA. But at AA they add, 'Keep coming back. It works if you work at it.' At NA we form a circle, hold hands, recite the saying, and then cuddle everyone in turn to illustrate our caring and sharing of our problems. At first it was a very emotional experience, and when we all cuddle it still brings a lump to my throat.

I have become very close to my AA groups. I give my private number to anyone who wants it both at AA and GA. I'm forever on the phone to a member of one of my groups. I get an average of ten calls a week, and they sometimes go on for hours. We can chat about anything at all, but the important thing is to care about each other, to want to know and want to help each other. And nowadays I try to help others myself.

I went to the top-security Swaleside Prison on the Isle of Sheppey to talk to the inmates in their group AA and NA meetings. A friend of my uncle was in there and my uncle made the arrangements with the warden. I talked to the prison alcohol and drug units.

It was an eerie feeling visiting the prison – it could have been me in there. When the doors locked behind me, it was a touch of sweaty hands for me! But once again this was a valuable reminder for me of what could happen to me if I ever went back to the booze. All I could hear was the banging of doors and clinking of keys. I was only there as a guest but it made me feel ill.

I told my story to the dozen members of the prison AA unit and the ten members of the drugs unit. I got some tremendous feedback, as they said I had been honest and blunt with them. I could relate to them so closely, I could have been part of that drugs units if I had stepped over that line.

It was a relief when I heard the prison door lock behind me as I left. It was a great feeling to be a free man. At the same time I got so much out of that visit. The warden rang my uncle and told him how well I had come across. I was delighted by that.

I had got used to press conferences by the time I was invited by the Football Association on 4 April to help launch their anti-drugs campaign entitled 'Fit For Football' alongside

England coach Terry Venables. This time I was in total control.

It gave me the chance I had wanted to warn youngsters against the evils of addiction. I made my point again that I hadn't used drugs in the run-up to a match, but with the drink and the other pressures, my game just went. It wasn't just using drugs and drinking – it was the mental worry and the fear. My confidence went and it just got worse, I explained, but at that talk at least I managed to laugh about it. 'Everybody could see that,' I said, 'you've only got to look at my Fantasy League points!'

The FA's anti-drugs campaign followed cases involving Crystal Palace striker Chris Armstrong, who tested positive for cannabis, and also two Charlton teenagers. Its message was backed up by a ten-minute video which featured Manchester United's Andy Cole and Blackburn's Alan Shearer speaking out against drugs. I described my treatment in the Southampton clinic as 'the best thing that's ever happened to me'.

It's still with me, and it's going to be with me for the rest of my life. It's just that I don't use drugs now, or drink or gamble. As long as I don't get involved in any of it, I'll be all right. Some days are hard and others aren't. But the hard days are a hundred times better than the good days I had when I was using drugs and drinking.

I receive about a thousand letters a week from people with drug, alcohol or gambling problems. I enjoy going out and talking to kids in schools and people in prison and telling them my story – the hell I went through and how good it is now. I got help, and now it's up to me to help other people. And if I can help just one person it's better than nobody at all.

Young players must get help immediately they think they have a problem. Whatever the FA want me to do I'll do it, just to help younger players. I have thrown a big part of my career away. I'm getting on now in football terms – I'm twenty-seven. I count myself very lucky. I was silly, I made a massive mistake. I was given a second chance, but I don't expect a third chance. To any younger kids who haven't started using drink, drugs or gambling, I'd say stay that way.

My ambition is to stay at Arsenal, win more trophies and to play again for England. Those are my aims now and they keep me on a high. I very badly want to play for England again – it's one of my dreams.

I was greatly encouraged when Terry Venables said how much respect he had for me for bringing these problems to the surface. And he suggested that my problems wouldn't go against me if he thought I merited an England call-up.

And I felt as though I was getting back to my peak as Arsenal won a place in the European Cup Winners' Cup Final, despite a very indifferent season partly as a result of the club's internal problems – one of which was me!

It was a magic night in Genoa when we beat Sampdoria in a dramatic penalty shoot-out – even though I missed a vital penalty kick! The champagne flowed in the dressing rooms, and there were wild scenes of jubilation. Nothing unusual in that. In fact, precisely what you would expect after the extraordinary heroics of that shoot-out. But of course I had to walk away from the bubbly. I couldn't go in there. How could I? A self-confessed alcoholic.

Even a penalty miss at such a critical time didn't have for me the meaning it might have had for any other footballer. When you've been through what I have, it puts a penalty miss into perspective.

When I missed that goal with so much at stake, I walked back saying my serenity prayer over and over again to myself: '...accept the things I cannot change.' All the way back to the halfway line I was putting that loss into proportion. I couldn't change what had happened, so I was minimizing the impact of it on my life.

But at least we were in the Final and I felt elated because I had always said that's what I wanted to do – pay everybody back.

I was just thankful to David Seaman and his hat-trick of penalty saves. It's always been the same at Arsenal – never give up, never say die, and in the end we fully deserved it. Their first goal shook everybody up, but we fought back. For Ian Wright to score again in the tournament, and maintain his record of scoring in every tie, was just phenomenal.

I survived a gruelling extra time period for the first time since my comeback. I was able to get through it, but only a short while ago I never dreamt I would ever be able to play extra time again.

Before the Final against Real Zaragoza in Paris I committed myself unreservedly to the club that has played such an enormous part in my rehabilitation. I have two years left on my current contract with Arsenal and I'd be more than happy to sign for life. I owe them so much.

As for playing in a major European final after all that had happened, that was unreal. I never dreamed this was possible. In fact when I first came out of treatment the first match I watched was the FA Cup-tie replay against Millwall, and when the team went out of the competition, I thought that would be it for the season. At that stage I couldn't even look ahead to another game, and now my dream had come true and I was playing in this European final.

Unfortunately we lost to a bizarre Nayim goal.

But even in defeat, I now realized that there are more important things in life. It was left to me to console the others, particularly the crestfallen Ian Wright and goalkeeper David Seaman, beaten by a fifty-yard lob from Nayim. In the past I would have been looking for someone to console me.

I certainly didn't blame David. He was beaten by the greatest goal I have ever seen. Pele tried it in the 1970 World Cup in Mexico and others have had a go since. Ian Wright tried it against Manchester United but no one has succeeded from that range until now. I saw Nayim look and take aim. It was perfection and something that I will remember for ever. Nayim was the only player who was going to do something like that, and I doubt if football will ever see a goal like it again.

Perhaps the hardest thing I had to endure was a week away on the end-of-season tour, away from Lorraine and the kids, and my therapy and group sessions. Arrangements were made for me to attend AA and GA counselling in Hong Kong. I spent my time woı king on my autobiography. I threw myself into this work and it has become part of my rehabilitation.

As soon as I arrived at the team's hotel in Hong Kong I was given counselling by one of the top psychiatrists, a friend of Dr Tate's. I was in the gambling and drinking capital of the world and under enormous pressure. We talked for an hour in my room and the counselling helped and I got through it.

That night I went out with the lads for a while. They couldn't believe the transformation. Of course they had been told that I was off the booze, but as always there were plenty of sceptics around. But there I was drinking my diet Coke while they were enjoying their lagers. It was the first time I had been out with them since I had been in treatment. They were amazed, but they respected me for what I had gone through to reach this stage. But they knew that a year ago I would have been on the booze. I knew what I would be like, out of my mind with the drink, applauding myself for being such a self-confessed idiot. I would be loud and obnoxious.

I stayed out no more than an hour or so with the boys that night. Most evenings I would spend alone in bed reading my books on GA, NA and AA to get me through the week and occupy my time. It had been arranged for me to attend an AA meeting in Hong Kong but it didn't materialize, as there was some mix-up. But if I couldn't go to a meeting, the books were the next best thing.

And of course I rang as many people as I could. Arsenal were very good to me, and agreed to pay my phone bill, whereas normally the players foot the bill for their personal calls. It was a great gesture, particularly as my calls must have come to around £1500.

Stephen Stephens, my counsellor back at Marchwood Priory, hadn't wanted me to be faced with such stress and tried to get my release from the end-of-season tour. He knew how hard it would be for me and made representations to Mr Friar at Arsenal. But he was told that it was part of the contract that I had to go and it was too late to avoid it. I asked to take my sponsor Steve along with me, and the club agreed, which was very generous of them, but there wasn't enough time to arrange a visa for him for China.

One of the lads got in trouble over drink in Hong Kong. I felt so sorry for Ray Parlour and I knew that there but for the grace of God... I've done what Ray did a million times, but I've never smashed anyone in the face before, although I can understand how easily it might happen. It showed me how I used to be and how I am now. It was another timely reminder about what still could happen to be if I ever relapsed. And, yes, I know it could happen at any time. It is something I learn in every group therapy meeting, something I repeat to myself all the time – 'I haven't yet been in prison, I haven't yet lost my family.'

The tour over, we arrived back home and the club's vice-chairman, David Dein, came over to congratulate me on 'a brilliant tour'. He said that I had coped very well and he was very pleased for me. Stewart Houston also came over to me and said that I had been a credit to myself and to the club. It was touching. Nobody ever said anything like that to me before! I felt proud.

The future. Well, who can predict the future? My aims are simple enough, to keep myself clean and have the courage to carry on the way I am. But the future in football is always totally unpredictable.

I was on holiday in Florida at the end of June with my family, playing golf, relaxing and feeling great, and then I heard the news that Arsenal had signed Dennis Bergkamp. Wonderful. A true star, and an exciting signing.

But then I learned that our new manager Bruce Rioch handed over the number ten shirt – the shirt I had worn at the club for eight years. However, once it had sunk in, I felt it was an honour to have given up my shirt to a world-class player. It's a tradition on the Continent that world-class stars wear the number ten. Pele, Maradona, Mattheus, Platini, Zico, Baggio and Zola have all worn that revered shirt.

I was relieved to hear that our new boss didn't hand it over as any slight to me! As long as I stay at Arsenal I don't care what number shirt they give me – so long as it's in the first team!

Maybe in the past I would not have been able to cope with that sort of pressure. Now I can. I've got much more confidence in myself. I've got my self-respect back. Bit by bit I'm regaining the trust of the people that matter most to me, such as Lorraine. My self-esteem is returning. I don't want to give it up. But I still have to take it a day at a time.

There is an old football saying, 'Put your medals on the table', and when I looked back at what I'd achieved – the medals, the honours, the England caps, the championships – I promised myself that I'd be back as good as before. But I came to realize there was only one way that I would achieve that, and that was to continue to go to my meetings religiously.

Everybody was convinced that I would be washed up and finished. I always believed that I was anything but washed up. I always planned to resurrect my career and you can't say I've done too badly in helping the team to reach the European Cup Winners' Cup Final.

I always felt it was totally wrong to look upon me as some sort of drop-out or loser. If I was a loser Arsenal would have got shot of me long ago. If I wasn't any use to the team they'd have sold me off. When I look at my career on the field, there's nothing wrong with that – my problems were all off it.

Apart from the European Cup I've won everything there is to win, and how many players can boast that? The Coca-Cola Cup, the FA Cup, two League Championships, the Cup Winners' Cup, Young Player of the Year, fourteen England caps. Does that look like a loser? I've done it, I've shown the qualities necessary for success, maybe in the past, but I know I could show them again. I hunger for success again, I want it desperately. My dream is to win the League again for Arsenal. The League is of paramount importance to every player.

Don't let anyone kid you that the FA Cup has all the glamour. It has glamour all right but you can win it in just six games and might not even play a Premier League team along the way. To win the championship it takes consistency at the highest possible level over forty-two matches, and you play each team twice.

I might have settled just for a comeback in the Arsenal team. But deep down I feel I will one day play for England again. My inspiration is the shining example of players like Ray Wilkins. He is someone I have admired throughout my professional career – in fact ever since I was a kid. Ray sticks out as the main man to look up to, a role model.

Perhaps I never will be like Ray because of my reputation, but I certainly don't see myself as self-destructive. True, there have been times when I felt like I was cracking up, times when I felt like packing it all in. In my lowest moments football didn't mean anything to me. But when I look back, I was never going to throw the rest of my life away. There was a phase I went through when I thought I'd achieved just about everything, but that only shows my immaturity. My very career is at stake at the moment and don't I know it.

I'm not one of these know-it-alls who thinks there's nothing left to learn in football or in life. I've got so much to learn it's unreal. I learn every day I turn up for training at Arsenal, and it's with that club that my priorities lie. I think that on my day I'm still good enough to play for my country. But I can't be thinking of England until I've fought my way back into the Arsenal team. It's a well-known fact that when you are playing well for your club everything snowballs from there and you have a chance of playing international football.

Playing for England is a long way down the road for me at the moment, though. My mind is back on track and I'm thinking about Arsenal and football again. Arsenal have stuck by me and I'm grateful for that – I don't know how I can ever repay them.

My life starts again from today. Now it's up to me to put the dark days behind me. Right now I'd just settle for playing well for Arsenal – in fact just getting into the team would do for me. You might think that because of all those things I've won I might be smug or self-satisfied. Far from it. I know I've got a long way to go before this stain is removed.

Besides a healthy respect for Ray Wilkins, I've also admired David Platt, because he has been involved in £16 million worth of transfers, has a dream career in Italy, and because he is captain of England. I am sure I can learn from the way he has handled his own football life. Platt's accumulative transfers have reached a world-record figure for an individual, but all I've got to show is a handful of England caps. Yet when I got into the England team I was playing well.

My best game ever was probably against Germany in America. In that match I hit the bar and if that had gone in it would have been some sort of wonder goal – and against the world champions at that. It wasn't a one-off performance either, for England. I did as much as anyone to try and get us to the World Cup Finals. I hit the post with a free-kick against Holland and also hit a shot just wide. I'm still two years away from being in my prime and I aim to get there.

That's the future.

AFTERWORD

by Stephen Stephens, STB, CAC

This book is but a chapter in the life of Paul Merson, and in the minds of many people there are still many questions yet to be answered. There are still more questions that are as yet unthought of that will only reveal themselves in the future as Paul faces the challenges of life as they unfold before him. In this sense he is no different from any of us. None of us knows what the future holds; nor can we predict how we will react in particular circumstances.

Some people may wonder whether Paul will ever use alcohol or drugs, or gamble again; others may believe that he is cured. It is certainly not inevitable that he will do any of these things again; nor is it inevitable that he will not. But to think in this way is to misunderstand the problem.

Paul sought help with an alcohol and drug misuse problem combined with compulsive gambling. In short he had what many call an addictive illness which had manifested itself in all these activities. If Paul had continued without seeking help it is highly probable that his illness would have developed until it eventually wrecked his career and his life. The fact that he sought help indicates that he realized that something needed to be done and that he could not resolve his problems alone. He recognized that he had somehow lost his ability to make constructive choices about alcohol, drugs and gambling.

Addictive problems are not planned – they happen; and usually they develop very slowly. They are confusing because the sufferer often has periods when he (or she) does not drink or use drugs or gamble. Naturally enough this leads the sufferer to believe that he is cured. He usually tries again, perhaps just one drink, and doesn't get drunk. Then, in the words of the old proverb: 'The man takes a drink, the drink takes another drink and then the drink takes the man.' At this stage the sufferer is back at the beginning, confused, guilty and wondering how he finds himself in this state again when all he intended to do was enjoy a few drinks. The sufferer finds that not only has he got drunk or stoned, or bet too much, but he has also broken promises to loved ones. This cycle results in everyone associated with him feeling let down and betrayed.

The goal of Paul's treatment was to break this destructive cycle. Although Paul had recognized that he could not drink, use drugs or bet without conflict, he could make decisions about what course of action he wanted to take. Having decided that he wished to cease these activities, he could put his energy into developing strategies that would help him achieve this goal.

On a daily basis Paul worked on identifying ways of dealing with issues that would enable him to live, one day at a time, a life free of alcohol, drugs and gambling. Today his problems in those areas are arrested. This means that they do not affect him in a destructive way; it does not mean that he is cured. In this way addictive illnesses are no different from many other medical problems. A person suffering from diabetes cannot be cured, but the problem can be arrested. In the case of a diabetic this is done through the use of insulin when necessary, and diet. When the correct regime has been worked out the sufferer follows a daily routine that addresses the problem. With careful monitoring, and if the sufferer follows the doctor's directions, it is hoped that the problem will not cause distress to that person again. There is no guarantee that the diabetes will not become problematic again. But if it does, the process is re-evaluated and new strategies are developed with which to address the new situation.

A similar approach is used to deal with addictive problems. A life plan is developed. In Paul's case this does not involve medication but it does involve his taking certain actions each day. Through this strategy it is hoped that Paul will never again suffer a relapse into addictive behaviour, but there can be no certainty about this. If problems should recur while he is following his regime then he has the best possible chance of dealing with them before the consequences become disastrous. This does not mean that a return to alcohol, drugs or gambling is likely. It is simply a recognition that relapse is possible.

Paul lives each day in the knowledge that he has to accept responsibility for the maintenance of his well-being. He has to ensure that he keeps himself mentally and emotionally fit by performing specific exercises. Some exercises he must perform alone, while others he shares with people who have suffered from similar problems to his. For Paul this type of routine is not unfamiliar. As a footballer he has to make sure that he remains physically fit. Each day he has to train – sometimes alone on personal fitness and at other times with his team. In this way he attempts to ensure that he is match-fit. The exercises he has learned and continues to practise to deal with his alcohol, drug and gambling problems are to ensure that he stays life-fit.

Just as a well-trained footballer, when match-fit, is not immune to injury, so a person who is committed to recovery from addictive problems is not guaranteed immunity in the future. All any individual can do is prepare well to face the challenges before him. If he does this, whether it be for sport or to combat illness, it is far less likely that things will go wrong.

Every footballer knows that each injury-free match is a bonus, and every person suffering from an addictive illness knows that every addiction-free day is a miracle. Neither the footballer nor the sufferer from addictive problems begins each day expecting problems, yet each realizes that if he is unprepared he runs greater risks.

Since leaving Marchwood Priory Hospital Paul Merson has taken his responsibilities both as a footballer and as a recovering person very seriously. He trains hard regularly, he listens to his coaches, and he shares his thoughts and ideas about football and his problems. He uses his experience of football and of addiction to assist others in their growth. If he continues to do this he can look forward to a very successful football career and a very healthy recovery. But in neither case can he afford to be complacent, as this would risk losing what he has worked so hard to gain.

At this point some readers may wonder whether Paul's battle has been a success or not. Some may conclude that it is, others that it is not, and both sides could probably put forward arguments to support their opinion. Yet ultimately it is Paul who must decide, as he is the only one who can really know the struggle and the emotional agony that he has had to face. It is only he who can decide whether it has been worth all the effort so far.

If Paul had been playing a football match instead of dealing with problems of addiction, the story may well have read that, after a bright start, the team seemed to lose its way. At this stage of the game they seem to have come to terms with the challenge and are definitely ahead. But this would be just part of the story, as leading at half-time or even seconds from the final whistle does not mean that the match is won. A true professional knows that he has to play until full time if he wants to win.

Today Paul realizes that he cannot take his recovery for granted; nor can safely make prophecies about the future. But he can look back on his life and reflect on which things have worked and which have failed. And he can use his experience to plan each new day. Today he can face life with a comfort and a confidence that he never possessed before. He can feel good about his accomplishments while at the same time being able to accept responsibility for past mistakes. Today Paul is a winner, but he must recognize that in terms of his life this is not even half-time, and the game is not over until the final whistle blows.

Paul is not cured but he is definitely well. He is growing in fitness – physically, mentally and emotionally. There are reasons to be cautious about the future, but more reasons to be optimistic.

In the forthcoming season I look forward to watching both Paul's continuing recovery and the development of his career as a footballer. It is my belief that, provided he continues to maintain his fitness in all areas, the best is yet to come.

AFTERWORD

For Paul Merson, as for all of us, each day is the first day of the rest of his life. He, like us, will have to make some difficult decisions. For Paul it is not so much a question of whether he will decide to drink or use drugs or gamble. For him it is knowing that today, unlike before, he can choose not to and can enjoy the freedom that this decision grants him. May he and all those who suffer from similar problems choose wisely.

LIVING WITH PAUL MERSON'S ADDICTIONS

Lorraine Merson

My life with Paul reached the stage where the tension was at such a pitch, the bickering so bad, that I'd truly had enough. 'You've got to go, Paul, I can't stand any more,' I told him. There had been times when I had told him to get out, but never really meant it. This time I meant it, all right. I just couldn't take any more. Paul might have thought I was messing around again, not really meaning it, but he had misjudged it this time. I just wanted him to say, 'I'm sorry, I love you, forgive me.' Just some sort of regret. Instead he would shout, 'Fuck off then if that's what you want, see if I care . . . and don't bother to come back.' He would often taunt me by screaming, 'It's my house, I'm not going anywhere, I've earned the money, I've paid for this house.' Paul's gambling debts were getting out of hand, he had gone too far, and he couldn't cope. I couldn't cope. At worst, I thought, he couldn't cope with his gambling debts. I didn't have a clue what was about to hit me in the next few weeks.

I had reached the point of no return. I'd taken all I could take. I had a terrible vision of how to make Paul stop gambling. I pictured him and the kids standing over my grave crying with Paul promising he would give up. I contemplated killing myself to make him stop, for the sake of the children, for their futures. Maybe I would finally get some sympathy from Paul if I had taken my life. Maybe he would show sympathy at my funeral. He'd tell me to 'fuck off' a hundred times in a day – it meant nothing to him; he had become unbearable.

I never told Paul about this until the day we drove to the publishers to talk about his writing a book and that they wanted me to write a chapter. Paul was staggered.

151

But he knew how angry I had become about the gambling when we had this furious row at home, and I told him to get out. The row continued as we went upstairs. 'Is that what you really want?' he shouted back. For the first time he could tell I wanted him out of the house and that I meant it. He came upstairs and began packing his bags.

He was just one big heap on the floor. He looked in a total mess, he didn't know what he was doing or where he was going. For the first time I took pity on him and thought to myself, this boy needs help! Something told me he was ill.

He turned round and blurted out, 'My life's not worth living, I'm no good to you, no good to the kids.' He was cracking up. He went on, 'I'm finished.'

Luckily Charlie was out of the house playing with his friends. I would have hated him to have seen his dad in this state – it was pitiful.

Well, if Paul thought his life was not worth living, what about mine? He didn't know what he was doing to me. Now I told him straight. 'What is happening to you? What are you doing to me?' If we were socializing, either in the house or in a restaurant, he would think nothing of swearing at me in front of everybody. But I'd take it, as if it wasn't important, as if it wasn't hurting me.

I knew he was suffering, he was ill, and that he needed some kind of treatment. I couldn't let him out of the house, shove him out in the cold. He was looking rough, so I told him to take some painkillers and get himself to bed.

A year earlier I went to Relate, in a desperate attempt to patch up a marriage that in reality was little more than a sham. You can imagine how bad it was for me to try marriage guidance, but let me tell you it was nowhere near as bad as it eventually got. I was recommended to Relate, which had a branch in St Albans, by a close friend, who had tried it; not successfully but she felt it might help and have some effect on my marriage. My relationship with Paul had gone steadily downhill to the point where we were plodding along but had little or no physical or emotional relationship. I confronted him about our problems and asked him to come with me to

Relate. I asked him a couple of times, but he didn't want to know. He refused point-blank, and actually became very aggressive about it. He shouted at me, 'You can go if you want. I'm not, I haven't got a problem.' That was the end of the conversation. In those moods there was no getting through to him, and it illustrated how he never believed that he had anything that needed some sort of treatment. And I was pretty much as ignorant as he was about just how deep were his problems.

I rang up and made an appointment and went along by myself. I told a woman counsellor there that my husband was a gambler and that it had wrecked our marriage. I purposely didn't mention the drinking. But I said that we had grown so far apart that I felt we were trapped in a loveless marriage and that I wanted desperately to do something to change it. I wanted advice on how I could make my marriage stronger and alter the fact that I felt I was living with someone, and still loving someone, who didn't love me and was showing me no feelings or respect.

I walked out of Relate thinking, what am I doing? I knew that this was not going to work. No matter how many times I went there it was useless unless Paul was going to cooperate and come with me. The advice I got from Relate was that Paul had to be part of the will to make the change, to find out the root cause of the problem and to do something to put it right – and that wasn't going to happen.

I told Paul of my visit to Relate. He just laughed. He shrugged it all off, making it perfectly clear to me that he wasn't the slightest bit interested. Whether he was or not, I don't really know. But I was convinced at the time that he didn't seem to care at all.

'Why should I be the one to try to make our marriage work' was Paul's answer. And, that was the end of that. He could be so stubborn, there was no way on this earth that I was going to make him change his mind. One of his strong points is his single-mindedness, but this was working against me and I knew I had no hope of making him change his mind.

Yet I felt it was a turning-point. My desperation had reached the lowest point. It began to dawn on me that there was nothing that could be done, unless there was some sort of catastrophe that would bring everything to a head, and then Paul had no choice. All I wanted from him was to show me some affection, to love me like he did when we first met. I would do everything for him, irrespective of how much he abused me mentally. I would do it no matter what, because deep down I still loved him. I never said, 'No, do it yourself', when I knew that really I should have done, and no one could have blamed me.

I suppose it was a turning-point, because it was the first time I really knew I was on my own. Relate was not going to resolve anything, and I had no one to turn to, but I also realized that I never wanted anyone else but Paul. I was lost.

A year later it was coming to a crisis, and I knew I had to shock Paul out of it, or do something to alter a situation that was simply drifting from bad to worse.

Although I thought I was doing the right thing, my decision to contact George Graham only served to heighten the tension. Totally unbeknown to Paul, I left the children with a friend and met George for a chat – and for help. It wasn't the first time I had met him. I had spoken to him five years earlier about Paul's gambling problems and found him very sympathetic and supportive and that's why I turned to him again. I knew Paul was in trouble and it was only a few weeks before his public confession that I realized the extent of his gambling problem and his huge debts. I desperately needed someone to talk to. I made a confidential call to George's secretary, Sheila, and he returned my call almost immediately. I told him I knew Paul had been cheating with his weight and he said he knew. We just talked and talked. He comes across as the hard figure in football but I have always found him totally supportive.

After that call I made a big effort to track Paul down because I wanted to tell him what I had done, and I felt it was imperative that we talked. I suppose I wanted to shock him, but more important I wanted to shake him into realizing what he was doing with his life and how it was wrecking our relationship and jeopardizing the future of our kids. I knew he would be livid that I had spoken to his manager. But I wanted to explain to him face to face how bad it had got to force me to do it. I eventually found him and over the phone begged him to come home and talk about it.

'Can't.'

That's about all he could say. But I could tell he was devastated that I had consulted George Graham for advice.

'Why can't you?'

'I can't because I'm screwed up.'

Charlie could hear all the commotion and was naturally disturbed and deeply upset, and wanted to talk to his dad. 'Please come home and see me, daddy,' he said.

'I can't come home, mate.' Paul was really cut up but he couldn't come back and face it.

Of course he eventually came back in the small hours, drunk. At least I thought he was just drunk.

But that was the night he took drugs and slept with that girl. I didn't have a clue again.

It wasn't the drinking as much as the gambling that had brought us to the brink several times. He has always been a gambler. As far back as four years ago, he would bet on football, the horses, everything. There were times when he would spend all Saturday plugged into Teletext to get the results. I used to go to bed but he'd sit up into the early hours for them. I caught him out once when I picked up the extension in the bedroom and heard him listening to the commentary for American football. It really worried me and I would get the hump, but I never knew how serious it was.

When Paul told me he'd once lost £20,000 on a bet, I just shook my head in total disbelief. I just didn't have a clue. It reached the stage where I didn't want to know. I was too frightened to find out. Paul ran up huge 0898 phone bills, but I didn't realize until the calls were itemized on the bill. We were getting bills of more than £450 a quarter. When I found out where the money had been going I confronted Paul, but he accused me of ringing British Telecom to check up on him. For a while afterwards he switched to using his mobile phone. He would always put bets on before he came home so I never realized how often he was betting.

Before he went to Gamblers Anonymous, the previous four or

five months were by far the worst. Paul had been very quiet, very short-tempered and very sharp with me. We just hadn't been able to communicate. He lived in a world of his own. I noticed this change of attitude, but I couldn't prove what had caused it. I tried to get him to sit down and talk about it, but he would just shrug it off. In the end I didn't even like to ask. I'm a very strong person and I realized I had to give myself some time.

The worst part was in May 1994, when Paul attacked me. He really frightened me, so I called the police. They didn't ask me if I wanted to press charges. I had no injuries anyway and it couldn't be proved in court.

They told Paul to calm down and said they would be back if there was any more trouble. He goes to football training in the mornings and used to come home. If I did not see him after training, then I wouldn't see him until the early hours of the morning. He used to come back and go straight to the spare bedroom. The funny thing was, in the morning he was always lively. I would never have let him get away with being hungover. I expected him to get up in the morning for the children. He would be full of apologies and would tell me he was giving up drinking and staying out late but I just took it with a pinch of salt. He would be a new person for a couple of days.

It was like having Mr Wonderful around the house – but then he would go back to his old ways. We argued all the time, mostly about his gambling, and about his attitude towards me. I seemed to be the person who ran his life but the one he least worried about. I was his little comfort, the woman who'll always be there. And I still am. There were many times when I just felt like strangling him. He would stay out all day while I was with the children, and he would think it OK, it's all hunky-dory. I have come close to kicking him out several times, but it's always in the heat of the moment and I soon forget. If I had wanted to leave, I could have stung him for every penny and taken the children and he knows that. But there is something else that holds me there with him. Perhaps I have been too soft. If he wanted to go out for a drink, then I never stopped him. You only have one life, so you should enjoy it. But his drinking became an embarrassment. We would go out to nice restaurants, and whereas I would sip a couple of glasses of wine he would order more and more beer and carry on way into the night. He just didn't know when to stop.

Paul has never seen me short of money. There were times when we struggled but we always managed. Paul would give me his last £100 and so there were no clues as far as money was concerned. I couldn't fault him on being a dad, either. He is a number-one father and has always spent a lot of time with the kids.

Once Paul phoned me from a pub and poured out his troubles. He was in tears, and told me of his heavy gambling and drinking. It was then that we decided to go to Gamblers Anonymous.

Paul was with me during the birth of our sons Charlie, four, Ben, two, and Sam, four months. Just after having Charlie and Ben, he seemed to pay no interest to me, and just couldn't wait to get out and get drink. It seemed to be another excuse to have a drink.

I had been cut a pretty harsh deal for a very long time, years, and I think you have to be a special person to suffer it and survive. But at the end of the day, I love Paul and it would take a lot now to break our marriage.

Let's face it, I had to suffer just about every torment that might have broken us up. The worst, of course, was when he owned up to sleeping with another women.

I must admit I was living in some sort of vacuum, unaware of what goes on out there and it was going to be some rude awakening. It began to worry me when the next thing was that Paul was ringing me from his friend Jerome's office and he told me he was there because he was doing an article for a national newspaper. Well, that was no big deal because he had put his name to articles before about his gambling problems. That left me a little confused. Why he was doing it again, at least why would a paper want to do it again? I kept on thinking his debts must be much worse than he'd been telling me.

Paul came home very late that night from Jerome's office in Edgware. He didn't want to talk about it, and he wouldn't talk about it. In the morning he just told me he would be going back to

Jerome's office after training again to finish off the article, and off he went.

The next time I heard from him he was about to turn my day, and the rest of my life, upside down.

It was all so much of a blur. He told me to get packed, that we might take the kids, we might go on our own, we might go to Florida, it might be New York, it might be, well, just about anywhere. Now I was really confused. You can imagine what was going through my mind. Anything but what was actually happening, I still couldn't imagine it. Why did we need to leave the country in such a hurry?

Paul was ringing me all day, telling me we had got to get out of the house, and get out of the country, and I wasn't having it, I kept telling him I wasn't going anywhere. I had no one to look after the children. The only way he was going to persuade me to do what he wanted was to get George Graham to do it. Paul obviously had rung his manager because when I got back from picking Charlie up from school there was a message on my answerphone to ring George Graham at his office. That was 4 p.m., and George explained what he felt was definitely for the best for us – that we should leave the country. I told him, 'How can I?' I tried to explain that I had the kids, I wouldn't know what to do with them, that I didn't want to take them with us. After all that was happening I didn't want to be miles away from the kids as that would have left me feeling even more isolated. What's more, at that point of our relationship I didn't want to go down the road with Paul, let alone out of the country.

But George pointed out that I had no choice. 'The press will be camping outside the house when the papers come out,' he explained. I couldn't quite take it all in, but I respected George's advice so I knew it was what I had to do.

I rang Paul at Jerome's office to find out precisely what he was up to. But again he refused to tell me until we were out of the country. I was frantic with worry. He told me to put just a few things in a case, and to tell Charlie he was going on a little holiday to my mum and dad's. I took Charlie and Ben to Paul's parents' house.

A *Daily Mirror* reporter, Jane Kerr, turned up outside the house.

Again I rang Paul and asked what I should do. Eventually it was decided to invite her in. Jane was there to take me to the airport. I called Paul's mum and dad and explained as much as I could and what was happening. They are great people and just said pack the boys' cases and they can come and stay here for as long as you need them to. They dropped everything to look after the boys and the boys thought they were going on a little holiday to nanny and grandad but they love the boys so much they would do absolutely anything to make sure they are happy. It also made me feel better because I know how much they love it there.

But first I had to take Charlie and Ben over to their house. It was very hard because all the way there Charlie was very inquisitive, and kept on saying, 'Where are we going mummy, are you going on holiday without me and Ben?' I just tried to explain to him that I just had to go away with daddy for a couple of days but when I got back I would bring him a present. That was so awful for me. I got to Paul's mum and dad's with the boys' cases, still not knowing where I was going. My mind was in a state of turmoil, and I felt heartbroken at the thought of leaving the kids behind. I had to walk away and leave them and I had never done that before, at least not for more than one night. It was dreadful.

But in fact the boys were fine. Paul's mum and dad were brilliant, and the kids loved it. They thought they were going on an adventure holiday to nanny and grandad's. It was just me who was cut up about it all. I was so stressed out by this time. I was in Jane's car on the way to the airport thinking, what the hell is my life coming to at this point? We went to the information desk and just sat there for forty minutes waiting to find out what was happening, where we were going. I sat there until 9 p.m. Finally Paul arrived with Bill Akass, another *Mirror* reporter, and we were off to Paris.

Halfway to Paris, sitting together on the flight, Paul said, 'I've got something to tell you.' I had a sick feeling in my stomach. He explained that a very controversial newspaper article was going to appear and that was the reason for all the rush to leave the country. There would be mayhem the next day. But I thought that he was able to cope with the press before, so why did he have to leave the country now?

Paul told me that he taking drugs. I said to him I thought the article was going to be about gambling. He said yes, it is to do with gambling as well. I said to Paul I think you've got your life into a bit of a mess at the moment, to say the least. He turned round and said he was going to sort it all out once and for all.

The first thing I wanted to know was whether he'd used drugs at home, in front of our children, and he said no. He told me that all the problems we'd been having were down to drugs. I had absolutely no idea. If anyone had asked me whether I thought he was on drugs I would have sworn on my life that he wasn't. I might have been naive, but I really didn't know. I knew nothing about drugs, didn't have a clue how it could affect someone's character, like the way it had affected Paul. I knew he loved a drink, I knew he loved a bet, I knew he loved to bet far too much and had run up huge gambling debts. But that was the extent of his problems as far as I knew. Drugs? I had no idea whatsoever. But in a funny way I was glad to hear something like this. At last there was an explanation for Paul's inexplicable behaviour. Even with hindsight I still can't remember a single time when I suspected him of taking drugs. I was worried about our boys and our families. But Paul tried to reassure me by saying he'd had enough, and that he was really going to stop. It took a lot of courage for him to come out into the open about it, and this time I really thought, he means it. He will stop. That gave me hope.

We checked into a hotel in Paris as Mr and Mrs Smith. We couldn't use false names on the air ticket because they had to correspond with our passports, and there wasn't time to sort that out. I was surprised that we could do something like that. But apparently hotels are very cooperative.

As soon as we checked in Paul looked around. He seemed very worried. Jane interviewed me and we talked until 2 a.m. in the restaurant. But things hadn't sunk in yet and I was very confused.

The next day the news had hit the TV screens and the papers. When I switched on Sky TV in the room, there was Paul. Everyone was talking about it. For the first time it really hit me. I thought to myself, this is serious stuff. They were discussing whether Paul should be banned, how long he should be banned for, and whether he should be banned for life. Naturally I was left wondering what was going to happen to us. It blew my brains apart.

I went down to the foyer to get away from the TV. I sat in reception for four hours. Bill was taking faxes from the office, Jane was wanting more copy for the newspaper and Arnie Slater, the photographer, was taking pictures of us wherever we went, whatever we were doing. Bill was very concerned. He wanted to keep us happy so that we would stay. But we were all worried that we would be caught out. To avoid detection we switched hotels, and also I was fed up being cooped up in the hotel close to Charles de Gaulle airport. It seemed that the whole thing was way beyond me and Paul and even to this day I didn't really appreciate just how big it was – a top player taking cocaine.

When we switched to a luxury hotel in the centre of Paris, I felt far more comfortable. The shops were close by and I had something to do. We had a lovely meal that evening, but I could tell by the look on Paul's face that there was something else he was keeping from me. He was still worried about being discovered. I began to feel like a fugitive on the run. Bill came with us everywhere. He had been with us to the shops and he was with us at the restaurant. The most free space he gave us was the length of a street! He would have a coffee and let us shop on our own but would meet up with us at the end of the road. In fact before we went out that day Paul spotted someone in reception who he was convinced was a reporter. He was paranoid about it. As we walked out, this guy followed us, and then ran down the street in the opposite direction. Paul was shocked, convinced that we had been tracked down. That evening in the restaurant, every time the door opened, Paul and I would automatically swing round to see who was coming in. I then knew how a criminal on the run from the police must feel. It seemed to me that we were on the run, and being hunted.

The next day, we left for the South of France and I began to feel much better. There were a lot of suggestions flying around where we would be safest. New York was one of the proposed destinations. But I was six months pregnant so I didn't feel it was appropriate to be dashing off to the other side of the world on a long-haul flight.

I had many happy memories of Paris, despite the hassle of trying to avoid detection. I began to see the change in Paul. Suddenly he was more attentive, more caring, and I had some good vibes about it all. I hadn't packed much because of the rush to leave and suggested to Paul that we ought to go shopping. In the past it was a nightmare to try to get Paul to go with me to the shops round the corner. I was surprised by his new attitude, a mood of cooperation. Naturally, I was very pleased about it.

We booked into the lavish Carlton Hotel in Cannes, where the Film Festival takes place; the sun was shining, although it wasn't particularly hot, but I began to feel a warm sensation as though we were making some progress in our relationship at long last. Bill and Jane allowed us the freedom of a meal on our own; I suppose they felt OK about it as we dined that night in the hotel. I felt as though I had been released from my prison sentence, that I was no longer on the run, that I could relax and unwind. We had a couple of glasses of wine, and that again surprised me, as Paul was already preparing himself to change his ways. We both knew that if he started on the lagers he wouldn't stop until he was under the table. But he wouldn't have had the front to sit there drinking lager in front of me. But it was still a shock to the system to see Paul drinking a couple of glasses of wine, taking alcohol in moderation.

Sunday morning Paul was a bit edgy. I could tell he needed to tell me something, but somehow, for some reason, he couldn't.

As the day progressed he became more and more irritable. He went to the gym for an hour's workout. He asked me if I wanted to come down and watch him, and told me he would get me anything if I wanted it. It all seemed too good to be true, Paul being so attentive. But I stayed in my room, and I didn't need anything. However, I did feel a little uneasy, but I wasn't quite sure why. Paul came back from the gym, and almost immediately said he had to go off to Bill's room to have a word with him.

When he came back, he was crying his eyes out. He blurted out that he'd had a one-night stand. I could barely make out his words through all the sobbing. But I just about got the gist of it. I felt so sick. Numb. I didn't feel like hitting him – I just felt betrayed. I really wanted it all to come to an end there and then.

After all that had happened I hadn't for one minute believed I was going to be hit with something much worse. And Paul had taken two days to make that confession. He knew how it would hurt me, and had wanted to postpone it for as long as he could. He was so worried that he told Bill to arrange the first flight out of Paris, as he was so scared I'd leave him on the spot, and never come back. At first I thought, you're right, I do want to leave right here and now. But then I thought, do I really want to go? I don't know how other people view me, but I'm sure I'm a thoughtful person, and once again I was thinking of Paul. How could I leave him on his own? How would he cope?

At the same time I was thinking about myself for a change. How could he do this to me after all I had done for him, and stood by him for so long? Surely I didn't deserve it? And why should I get on a flight on my own, six months pregnant and left to face the press and TV people on my own from the minute I set foot back in the country? The press would have sniffed out the story that I had returned on my own, and they would have guessed that it was because of a break-up with Paul once he had told me about the one-night stand. It would have been sheer hell for me with every paper chasing me about all the stories of possible divorce and refusing to stand by him.

It made sense to stay. We were originally due to stay abroad for a week, but it had been decided that Paul had to return early, so we were now due to return on Tuesday. I decided to stay until then, but I was glad we were going back earlier than had been originally planned.

When Paul told me that cocaine had led him to sleep with the girl, well, I was still trying to come to terms with his cocaine-taking and the fact that he was in danger of throwing such a brilliant football career down a pothole.

My initial reaction was, 'You bastard!' Yet somehow I never

thought it would be the end of our relationship. It should have been, because I had always said to him, and indeed to myself, that if I ever caught him with another woman that would be us finished.

Perhaps it was because I could finally see some light, some reason for all that had been happening. Perhaps I knew that he was going to change, that he was going to get treatment. Now I knew there was a real problem, I was sure there must be some kind of treatment.

There I was, so loyal, suffering so much because of his problems. I had never said, sod it, I'm off for a night out with the girls. I could have done that. Who would have blamed me after everything he had put me through? But I never thought about another bloke, I never looked at another man, and now I find out he's been unfaithful. I had been living with a man who had treated me like this, like a piece of dirt, and I had stayed loyal. Over the years, all the time we had been married I'd been out on a girls' night-out maybe half a dozen times, no more than seven times. But never to a disco. Never looking for men. Just a quiet meal, sometimes maybe not so quiet, but nothing other than a meal out. After all the hurt he caused me, why shouldn't I have flirted a bit? He would have deserved it. Yet I did nothing to hurt him.

Throughout our marriage Paul was always very protective of me, very guarded, very jealous. He wouldn't have been very happy had I gone out. But with men the arrangement doesn't seem to work in reverse. I never believed he would have done that to me. I was devastated. Once Paul had told me about the girl I had a strong urge to get back home as soon as possible to see the boys.

I had to talk to someone, but we were under instructions to talk to no one and certainly not to give anybody, no matter how close, any clue to our whereabouts. But I had to call Margaret and Stan, my mum and dad. They were the people who cared for me and who would be able to help me. They were devastated and heart-broken. Mum cried her eyes out. She could hardly speak. 'I'm just sick, Lorraine, I can't believe he's done this to you.' She had been shocked by what she had been reading in the papers, and refused to really believe any of it until she spoke to me. She tried to reassure me, saying, 'Don't get yourself upset.' All those times my mum and dad had come over to visit us or we had gone to them, they never suspected anything was wrong. How could I spill the beans, even to my mum and dad? I'm their only daughter – it must have been heartbreaking. And what would have happened if I had ever told them? They would have come over to sort Paul out – that would be the reaction of any mother or father to their daughter's situation.

All the time I had protected Paul, even though I had a shit life, and now I find out about this. Over the years I had covered up for Paul. I tried to make our relationship seem normal whenever we came into contact with family and friends. Basically I pretended. I was very good at it because no one suspected anything was wrong at all. I never confided to anyone. Not even my mum. And when I shouted at Paul because the stress had got too much, my mum was mystified and would tell me to 'calm down'. I just carried on living a lie. The truth is I would have been embarrassed if anyone had known.

Naturally my mum and dad were shocked at what was going on and that I had left the country. Naturally they wanted to know where I was. But I couldn't tell them. I could imagine the hurt they would be suffering when all of this emerged in the papers and they would have to go to work and face their friends.

That night we went out for a meal. It was not the same as the night before, when we'd been happy. The reality of what was happening started to sink in, once the shock of the confession wore off. I came to terms with it all by telling myself it was just a one-night stand, he didn't love that girl, he didn't actually have any sort of an affair, and it was because he had been drunk and stoned out of his head.

I asked Paul a couple of questions about it because I wanted to know exactly what had happened. I had to know that he didn't have a 'bit on the side' for any length of time. That would have been even harder for me to accept. He swore to me that it was only a one-night stand, and only the one girl. I always believe that you are responsible for your actions, and that you really know what you are doing. But I had been confronted by the fact that he was drunk and stoned. It didn't mean I forgave him – perhaps I never will – but it was possible for me to accept it because he was not in love with the girl, and his love is precious to me.

On Monday we went shopping. I was trying to come terms with everything, and the shopping trip was nice. That evening Bill and Jane went to great lengths to book us into a lovely restaurant in Monaco. They clearly felt sorry for me and wanted to give us a good night out.

I ate the starter and began feeling very sick. It certainly wasn't the gorgeous food. I started shaking, my legs were trembling and I had to lie down. I said to Paul that I would have to go outside for some fresh air before I collapsed. Paul immediately came out and said he wanted to call for a cab and take me back to the hotel. But I felt bad about ruining Bill and Jane's evening.

It had all caught up with me. I was six months pregnant and I couldn't take any more. I had just experienced the worst days of my life and had kept strong throughout this ordeal, but now I just wanted to go home and see the boys. I was so thankful that we would be going back the next day.

Paul took me back to the hotel, while Jane and Bill stayed on at the restaurant. I went straight to bed, and fell asleep immediately. The next morning we packed and although I couldn't wait to get home, I felt extremely nervous about what would be awaiting us back in England. Throughout Paul's career I had stayed well and truly in the background. I never wanted to be seen out as Paul Merson's wife. I didn't really want people recognizing me in the street and pointing at me. I feared that was all going to change.

When we were on our way home I realized I could not live without Paul, and Paul knew he could not live without me. That's what kept us together. We needed each other, and we needed each other to get us through this crisis. I knew Paul would have to leave me for a while to get treatment. But I wanted him to get help and I knew he wanted to be treated.

When Paul and I stepped off that plane I began to realize how Lady Di must feel being hounded by the media! We'd only taken two steps and there must have been twenty photographers in front of us, their lights flashing in our eyes. They were running backwards to keep up with us, shouting, swearing, jostling to get space for a picture. It was mayhem. A couple of policemen were there to shepherd us to the safety of Customs, where the photographers could not follow.

The funny thing was that the photographers thought Jane was Paul's wife to start with!

We went straight from the airport to Highbury. I saw Ken Friar and George Graham, and had a chat with both of them. They were so supportive about Paul's problems. I was taken to Paul's parents' house to be reunited with the boys, while Paul had to stay at his aunt's to avoid the media camped outside our house. The next day Paul attended a press conference, and we met up after that at his mum and dad's.

He explained he had to go away for treatment, but he didn't know precisely how long. Maybe eight weeks, maybe longer.

Oh my God, I thought. I didn't know how long we would be apart, or what was going to happen to him. Everything became a blur. So much had happened in the last week, there was so much to take in, and now this.

Yet at the same time there was something telling me this was right for Paul. He needed help, and I needed space, to be on my own to work everything out. But for Paul I knew that hospital was the best place for him, to sort him out. His career was on the line, and the FA had decided this was the best course of action for him. They knew that a ban would not help him, and would destroy him. I would be left on my own, but I would have to get on with it the best I could. It wasn't as if there was a choice: It had to be this way, and I accepted it, and so did Paul. In fact we both came to terms with it quite quickly.

Out of respect for my parents, I insisted that Paul come round to them the night before going into hospital, to explain everything to them personally. I felt he owed them that at least. We went together to their place. My mum and dad are both very understanding people, and they very supportive to Paul, which I know he appreciate. But they were understandably worried about how I would cope. They think the world of Paul. My mum says that he is the type of boy you simply cannot hate, there is such a nice side to him. Although there wasn't much of that 'nice side' that I had seen for many years, they were prepared to give him all the support and sympathy he needed to get himself better.

My mum rang her supervisor at work (she works in catering in a hospital) and was given six weeks off, which was fantastic. In fact they told her to come back when she was ready. Of course they knew about Paul's problems.

My mum stayed with me all the time Paul was away. She was the rock on which I survived it all.

That night I stayed at my parents, Paul with his as they were not far away. On Friday morning I drove him back to our house, where he packed all his stuff; not very much, a couple of pairs of jeans and bits and pieces. We had a chat and there were no sour feelings about what Paul had to do. He could have screamed and shouted that the whole thing was ridiculous, but he knew he needed help.

Paul couldn't wait to get there. Yet at the same time, he was naturally very apprehensive. It was heartbreaking to see him go. Around lunchtime Jeff Weston arrived to take him down to Southampton. He set off with his case not really knowing what to expect. It must have been hard for him. I said goodbye and he promised he would ring as soon as he could. I tried to be as strong as I could be for him. Then I picked up the boys from Paul's mum and dad, and for the next six weeks Charlie and Ben would hardly see their father. I felt very very sad for them, but naturally I told them daddy has gone away to pay football and he will ring them soon. I then picked my mum up, to drive to our house, and as soon as I saw her I felt a little stronger. I don't know what I would have done without her. I'm not the type who like to live on their own and I had visions of being left to look after the two kids alone, without daddy around. My mum has such a big heart, and it wasn't easy looking after me and the kids for such a long time. And my dad is also a wonderful person. He had accepted it, straight away, that my mum could leave. He was quite happy to look after himself for as long as was needed. What a great dad because he was left to get on with his work as well as look after the house on his own.

On his first day at Marchwood Priory Hospital, Paul met his psychiatrist and counsellor, and then rang me. He immediately burst into tears. He explained me that he asked them if he could be allowed home for Christmas and they said no. He felt shattered, heartbroken and let it all out when he rang me.

I told him that if it meant bringing the kids to the hospital for Christmas and staying there, than that is what I would do. I told him the most important thing that ought to occupy his mind must be his treatment. There would be years of Christmases after that. But I could imagine how isolated he must have felt, so far away from me and the boys, and suffering. When I came off the phone I started sobbing my heart out. Emotionally, everything had caught up with me, and I cried myself to sleep that night thinking about how sad it had all been for me.

This was a very vulnerable time for me as far as my emotions were concerned. At first I didn't want to see anyone. I was afraid to leave the house, to feel the fingers pointing at me. But I was encouraged by all the letters. I was so grateful for all my close friends and family who wrote letters of support. I even got fan mail. My mum and dad also got messages of support. When my dad went to work he never faced any hostility towards me and Paul, only people asking how his daughter was coping and passing on their best wishes. I was so grateful for all of this, and it helped me to want to face the world again. I felt everybody out there was rooting for us.

The first hurdle was taking Charlie to school. I kept postponing it and postponing it, but it wasn't really fair on him. He'd already been off school for a week while we were in France, and it was the best part of a fortnight before I plucked up the courage to go out and take him to school. I rang Charlie's teacher, Carol Erwin, and she was marvellous about it. She reassured me that all the parents and the teachers were behind me, and that they cared about our welfare and were thinking of us. She also explained that it was important that Charlie should get back to school.

Even so, it was a daunting task to face up to all those mums for the first time. Yet my fears were totally unfounded. Not one of them said anything to me, or asked anything about what had been happening. I'm sure they must have been curious about how I was coping, but it was just like any other morning, their attitude towards me the same as always. They saw me walk down the drive to the school with Charlie and I could sense that everyone was really pleased to see me. I've no doubt that they must have been thinking all sorts of things after all the stuff they'd been reading in the papers about me and Paul, but they kept it to themselves. 'Hi, Lorraine, how are you?' That was all they asked.

I had dreaded the first day, but after that everything was all right. At least it was at school and with my friends. And I was able to take Charlie to school every day without any worries. But not everyone was sympathetic.

Paul had been away about a week when some 'clever' people turned up in the dead of night at our house. We were all in bed but I remember that night I was a bit restless and had got up for a drink of water. I looked out of the small window by the front door and, still half asleep, thought it was snowing because I saw this white stuff on the grass.

In the morning when I looked out I was horrified to see a line of white powder from the front door to the edge of the drive and extending on to the grass. I opened the front door and felt sick. Hurt. Disgusted.

There are some sick people out there. Sad people! Unfortunately there was nothing I could do. Some jokers had put down powder of some kind, and must have thought they were being funny. But they never turned up again. Fortunately I wasn't on my own, otherwise it would have been far more traumatic.

I just washed it all away and tried to forget about it.

But I did decide to call the police when the local paper decided in their wisdom to publish an article about Paul and myself – and said where we live. The paper was published on Friday and by Sunday there were numerous cars driving up to the house and then driving away. They were just being nosy. I contacted the police to make a complaint about the paper's irresponsible attitude, but they said they couldn't do anything about it.

Paul was in regular contact, ringing as many times a day as he could, and was really looking forward to seeing me and the boys. I couldn't face taking the boys down to see him the first time. I wasn't strong enough because I couldn't cope with the awful prospect of reuniting them with their dad and then, within hours, taking them away from him.

Charlie was so excited about a trip to see his dad, even though he hadn't really noticed that he had gone missing. The mere nature of Paul's career kept him away from home for long periods, so Charlie was used to it, and his father's being away so long because of his treatment hadn't affected him. Paul would speak to Charlie on the phone from the hospital, but Charlie never asked him when he was coming home. Thank God he didn't. I don't think Paul could have handled that in the early stages. I had told Charlie that Paul was away as usual playing football. So when Charlie was told he'd be going to where daddy was staying, he naturally thought he was staying with the rest of the Arsenal team. He became really excited. 'Can I play football with David Seaman?' 'Will Ian Wright be there?' Charlie was thrilled to think he was going to see the whole team.

Paul had been having treatment for some time by now and he told me that he could no longer lie to Charlie. He said it was time to tell him what was happening, and not leave him believing he would be going to see the entire Arsenal squad. 'Daddy's been a naughty boy and he's had to go away to hospital,' he told Charlie, who accepted it, and nothing more was said.

Paul was not allowed any visitors for the first week, but because he had made such good progress he was permitted visitors at the weekend and he wanted to see the boys. But I just told him, 'Sorry, I'm not strong enough to bring the boys down.' He understood my feelings. Paul's mum and dad took the boys to see him on Saturday. Paul had a lovely day with the boys. They were so pleased to see him, and it perked him up a lot.

I went to see Paul with my mum and dad on Sunday with Paul's sister Louise, but without the boys. In the morning I stopped on the way at a petrol station and picked up the papers. There was an article by one of Paul's family. It was dreadful. I felt sick. I was just getting strong and coming to terms with everything that had been happening and then I opened the paper to see yet again pictures and an article about us. I tried to forget it all on the journey down, and by the time I got there I was just looking forward to seeing Paul.

When we arrived at Marchwood Priory, we walked down the corridor towards Paul and I was shocked when I saw him. He had only been away for a week, but the difference in his features was astonishing. His face was alive.

What a contrast to a week earlier when I sent him off to have his treatment and he looked so drawn and bedraggled. Now he looked the picture of health.

But I had a sick feeling when I went into his room. Everything was screwed down. It was so awful, but everything had to be secured in case anyone came back from therapy or group sessions and took their anger out by smashing their room up. I just wandered how he could stand it in there.

It was a tiny room, and very functional. The bed was in the air, raised on metal poles. Everything in the small bathroom was also screwed down. But Paul looked as though he had got himself organized; there was his pad and paper on the table, some sweets, and bottles of Perrier. I had brought him a few things to make him feel more at home. He asked me to bring him a duvet and a pillow as the covers were not what he was used to.

The first few days were hell for Paul. I've just got to get out of here, he was thinking. But by the time I visited him, which was only a week after he arrived, he had come to terms with his new environment and accepted that his sole purpose for being there was to sort himself out.

We had Sunday lunch in the dining hall. The food was fine. Paul never once complained about the food, although he missed his favourite Chinese and Indian take-aways! He was eating more than he had ever eaten before – regular meals, three times a day – and was looking much healthier. We went back to his room as his doctor wanted to meet me. Dr Austin Tate introduced himself and we all had a chat, and then he asked me if I could go to his office for a private talk.

Dr Tate asked me if I thought Paul was an alcoholic.

'No,' I replied.

'Why?' he asked.

Well, I said, he doesn't drink seven days a week, and I always thought an alcoholic was someone who woke up in the morning and had to have a drink. I wouldn't have said he was addicted to drink, although I would have said he was addicted to gambling had he asked me that.

Then Dr Tate explained to me precisely what constitutes an alcoholic.

'Yeah, he is an alcoholic!' I agreed.

He asked me a lot of other questions, but before he could finish I broke down in tears. He said he was really glad that I cried, as it showed great strength to be able to show your true feelings. He's a lovely man and I felt reassured that Paul was being cared for by such a well-qualified person.

It was Charlie's birthday the following week. It would be nice, I thought, for Paul to come home, particularly as he wasn't able to come home for Christmas. I asked if he could be released for the birthday party. I was told there wasn't much hope of that, although because he was making such good progress and showing so much determination and responding so well to treatment, it might be possible that he would be allowed home for Christmas. But that was not a promise, Dr Tate explained. This was great because it gave me a little hope and I knew it would make Paul feel happy to know he was progressing well.

I went back to Paul to tell him the good news that he might be allowed out for Christmas, and that brought a lovely smile to his face. He was so delighted because just a week earlier he had been told there was no chance of a homecoming for Christmas.

We had another chat in Paul's room until it was time for our goodbyes, and that was hard. But for Paul's sake I tried to be as strong as I could. I was glad that my mum and dad were with me to keep me company on the journey back home otherwise I might have broken down, particularly as I would have picked up the boys and returned to an empty house on my own.

But I knew that Paul was in the best place for him, and that one day he would come out a different man from the one that went in. And Paul kept in touch, ringing me endlessly, reading me his diary, crying down the phone if he had a bad day in counselling. I tried to give him as much support and encouragement as I could. I would just tell him, 'Work at it, and you'll get better.'

Paul had done so well he had been told he might be able to go home for Charlie's birthday. In the next week, just like the previous week, he showed such determination and willingness to work that he was given permission to go home for the occasion.

We were so glad that it worked out that way. It was so hard for Paul when Charlie was crying on the phone; that really touched him. My dad, Stan, picked Paul up from the hospital, and that gave them a chance for a long chat. When he explained to my dad that he could never drink again, Stan understood what he had been through and why we had so many problems. Paul realized the sort of things he was in danger of missing out on when Charlie's birthday took place that Sunday at the local hall. But Charlie was on cloud nine to see his dad. Although the food at the hospital was fine, Paul really missed his take-aways, so I cooked him a curry. We had a lovely weekend and Charlie's birthday went brilliantly. The boys just loved to see Paul at home even though it was only for one night.

It was a very emotional time for me when Paul had to return to Southampton. But every weekend after that he was allowed home. It became a very pleasant routine, Paul arriving around 3-4 p.m. on Saturday and leaving around 6 o'clock on Sunday evening. The only drawback was the amount of washing and ironing before I sent him back to Southampton!

Paul was later allowed home for Christmas, and that was so special to him. The day before Christmas Eve I received a bouquet of flowers, delivered by Interflora, from the Professional Footballers Association with 'best wishes for Christmas and the New Year, from everybody at the PFA'. I was touched by that. It shows you just how people do really care and I felt very warm inside to know that they were thinking about us and hadn't just pushed Paul away to sort out his life alone.

This Christmas was a bit special. Paul arrived home at 4.30 on the afternoon of Christmas Eve. It was so lovely to see him home. That evening we just prepared the kids' toys for the big day. You could see from the look on Paul's face that he was thoroughly enjoying every minute as this was the longest period he was at home during the treatment.

Christmas Day was great. Paul spent all day playing with the kids and their toys, but you could see by the end of the day he realized he would have to go back early in the morning to the hospital and he was already getting a bit upset about it. The kids had a wonderful day and Paul put them to bed.

Paul was up and out of the house by 7.30 on Boxing Day, before the kids woke up. My dad took him back to Southampton and it was a very emotional farewell as we had had a lovely weekend and the kids wouldn't know until they woke up that daddy had gone again. The kids woke at 8.30, brokenhearted to find that they hadn't got their dad to play with. I did my best to cheer them up, and they soon accepted it, as kids do.

The weeks passed and the day was drawing near when Paul would be let out. About a week before his release Paul spent a day at Highbury undergoing a series of assessments and meetings. That's when I first met his counsellor, Stephen Stephens. He asked me a few questions, and explained quite a few things to me.

He told me that Paul will never be cured. But if there was any consolation there was light at the end of a very long and dark tunnel for us both; it was not all gloom and doom. The bottom line was that the problem would be with Paul for the rest of his life, but that he can fight it.

Now it's as if I've known Steve Stephens all my life! He has become a constant source of encouragement for Paul, someone he can always rely on to contact and help him. He probably knows more about Paul than I do! Steve is a wonderful man and I care so much for him.

He had opened up my eyes. After eight years he made me realize and come to terms with Paul's addictions.

I was also told that I had a problem! Mandy, who is my sponsor, first told me this. I couldn't believe it. If anybody had told me that I had a problem all these years I would have said that cannot possibly be; I'm not a gambler, I'm not a drinker. It was really hard to come to terms with. But Mandy explained that living with a problem meant that I had a problem too, and that I would also have to go to counselling.

Mandy is such a loving, caring person, who has had to face a lot of problems in her own life. She gave me so much love and support through such a hard time, and showed me just how strong people become when they learn to come to terms with their problems and accept them. She would contact me every day to see how I was getting on and how I was feeling. She would take me out with her husband Steve, who is Paul's sponsor, for a meal. Mandy then made me realize that after all the problems she had encountered she was still married. After all, people with the smallest problem may end up divorced, but people who are strong and stand up to their problems with their partners, no matter how great, really can make it work.

The first hurdle was Paul's release. His six weeks were up, but he was kept waiting a bit and didn't know when he could go until the morning of his release. He found the waiting a bit hard. But I told him another couple of days won't change anything. He was in a counselling group when Stephen Stephens walked in to interrupt and told him to pack his case – he'd be leaving in an hour. Paul ran back to his room, packed and loaded up the car.

The pressure from the media was building up. There were people outside our house and a couple parked around the corner. I went out and told the reporters parked in the drive, 'Do you mind moving off.' They joined their colleagues in the main road.

Paul had to avoid the mêlée outside our house, so I took his suit around to our friends nearby. He then drove there to get changed.

Paul went to his press conference, where he broke down. He rang me on a mobile phone once the press conference had finished, to tell me it was being screened live on Sky TV. I immediately switched on the television and they showed Paul and I could see just what it was like for him. Someone asked him a simple question about what it was like being in rehabilitation for six weeks. He broke down, and I cracked up. I couldn't hold back when I saw him in tears. It was so upsetting that I started crying too. So did my mum. No one knew what Paul had been through, and when he was asked it triggered off all the emotions and memories of hardship he had been through. Who could blame him for crying? I think that made people realize he had a problem and how much he suffered for those six weeks, and that not many people would have coped with the problems that had confronted Paul in his life.

The next morning it was decided by the Football Association and Arsenal to allow a small group of photographers into the house for a family picture. The idea was to stop photographers following our every movement to take pictures.

What I didn't realize at that time was the extent of treatment that Paul needed, and how important a role I would have to play. My task is to encourage Paul to go to his meetings, but that didn't take much encouragement as Paul never needed any pushing to go. It's part of his lifestyle now and he is prepared to just get on with it. He attends Gamblers Anonymous, Alcoholics Anonymous and Narcotics Anonymous, and I attend the corresponding meetings for the partners.

GamAnon is the partners' equivalent of Gamblers Anonymous. I go with Paul to the same building, at the same time, but our meeting takes place in a different room. Paul goes with his sponsor Steve, and I go with my sponsor Mandy. I got a very warm welcome from the group when I first arrived in the room, as everyone is in the same position as me, and they were just so warm and welcoming, making me feel as though I had known them for a long time.

The group consists mostly of wives, but there are also parents of victims of gambling and alcohol abuse. Of course not everyone wants to talk about the problems they are experiencing, and it was difficult for me on the first night to express myself to the group. And when I first went and was told the identity of the people you see and what you hear doesn't go beyond the room, it made me feel very secure.

It was a huge help having Mandy there. Steve and Mandy are close friends, and both have experienced this sort of problem. Mandy had been attending GamAnon for eight years and that took an enormous amount of pressure off me, as I realized it must have worked for them as they couldn't keep coming back otherwise! Also, on my first session there wasn't a room full of complete strangers, which would definitely have made for a harrowing time. Mandy had been able to tell me what to expect. Now I feel that if you are living with someone who has a problem it is not just them that need help, but you as well. In addition, I did not feel as though I was on my own and that meeting other people at the group helped to lessen my loneliness and suffering.

Even though Mandy had warned me what to expect, I was still taken aback when I first walked into that meeting. It's a weird feeling, so strange, awkward, uneasy, all those strange, inquisitive faces looking at you. But my worst fears were not realized. It didn't turn out to be like that at all. In fact, they were warm, welcoming people who have also turned out to be very supportive and caring.

Possessions, wealth, any trappings of success – they are all meaningless, worthless, when you walk into that room. It doesn't matter if you have £1 million or £10, or nothing. It's irrelevant, because if you have £100 and you bet £100 you have nothing, and if you have £1 million and bet £1 million you still have nothing. Everyone there is equal.

GamAnon's group therapy teaches you how to cope. The secret is to let go. The idea is to give yourself some space, not to become obsessed with the idea that every time your partner is out of the house or on the phone he is placing a bet. The aim, when you are living with a gambler, is quite simply to let go, and not to blame yourself or feel that it's your responsibility to make him stop, but to leave that to the experts. The reality is that you cannot help a gambler no matter how much you worry about him. To learn to let go was such a great help to me. I no longer felt guilty for Paul's actions, I no longer blamed myself, and in fact I no longer blamed Paul.

It reached a stage with Paul when I knew that every time he walked out of the door he was going to put a bet on. Because he was in the public spotlight I always feared everyone would find out just how much he was betting; that seemed inevitable. Now it's totally different. As long as he goes to his Gamblers Anonymous meetings I am confident that he won't have a bet.

Some people in GA relapse and go back to gambling. I don't believe that Paul will succumb to temptation again. Of course there is no guarantee, and Paul has had one or two bad days, but he has come through them. I admire him for that. He has done wonders, and you have to commend him for his courage. He has come through a torturous course and shown remarkable determination. It is a route to salvation by stages, and after putting up with all the pain and tears, it would be a tragedy for Paul if he ever cracked.

First of all Paul had to come to terms with his problem, see it as a disease, not a recreation. The second step was to accept the problem for what it is. Paul has worked hard on all his steps. A lot of people don't make it, but he came to terms with his problems straight away.

Paul has come to realize the hard way that gambling is a bad disease that eats your money away, causes intolerable stress and can wreck your marriage, career and entire life. And in addition the drinking became uncontrollable. I have lived with Paul's gambling and drinking for eight years, so I should know.

Every time I confronted Paul he would snap, 'What are you talking about? It's not your money, I'm the one who goes to work to earn. I can do what I want with it.' He would lecture me about the finances, how the house had been paid for, how the mortgage was being paid, that we were never in mortgage arrears, how all the bills were paid on time every month. And in truth Paul never left me short of money. He always made sure I had money for the kids and food. I never wanted for anything because he always saw to it I had everything I needed.

I don't know how he managed it, because every spare penny went on his gambling, and he began running up huge gambling debts. Because he was Paul Merson superstar soccer player, he could always get plenty of credit. Everyone thought he was making enough to cover his debts, so we didn't seem to be suffering financially. Of course we were, because we were left without any money and only gambling debts. Had it gone on any longer there would have been the risk of big financial problems, and no doubt that sort of pressure was building up on Paul.

Now I feel that I have been asleep for eight years, and suddenly I have woken up. I knew Paul couldn't stop gambling and drinking, but I didn't want to split up. I had lost touch with reality. I actually thought my life was normality, that this must be happening in everybody else's marriage. It cannot possibly just be me and Paul, I thought. Surely this is the norm. But eventually it eats away at the fabric of the marriage, the strain becomes too much. It reaches breaking point.

Paul couldn't go a day without a bet. And he would simply lie to me. But I knew his moods swings inside out. I knew when he had won and when he had lost. One day he'd come in on a high and ask how the kids were and want to know what I'd been doing and what was going on. He was the perfect dad. But if he'd lost, the shit would hit the fan! All I would get was a full-blown argument about nothing in particular, followed by wholesale abuse.

Paul deluded himself that gambling didn't affect his football. But I was convinced that it did. I had been with him since we were fifteen. I watched him when he played in the Arsenal youth team, and followed him through the reserves to the first team. I never missed a game in the first four years of his professional life, although I had to slow down when I had our first boy, Charlie. The point is that I know Paul's game inside out and I would sit there in the stands and know that he was not the same player. I knew when he was a flop, and I told him so. 'What are you frigging playing at?' I'd say to him. But it didn't seem to have much effect. All he would say is, you're not the manager, so shut up.

There seemed to be something drastically wrong, and I put it down to Paul's gambling. I could see he was throwing his career down the drain, but I didn't realize his whole life was heading down the plug-hole as well. And at just twenty-six. It didn't bear thinking about. I told him he had a lovely wife, lovely kids, just about everything you could want, and a great career that looked as though it was about to end. Why throw it all away?

But I was powerless over him. He would tell me to shut up and fuck off if I didn't like it. He would tell me he was popping out to get a video but in reality he was going to have a bet. He would make any old excuse so that he could call in round the corner at the bookmaker's. He would create an argument so he could walk out and dash around to the pub. He would literally do anything to have a bet before going to work. He'd even volunteer to drop Charlie off at school because it would give him the chance to place a bet. He would be a little late coming back from training and tell me he'd been sitting around having a cup of tea with the lads. But I'd discover the Racing Post tucked down the side of the seat in the car, and know he had been in the betting shop. But when I confronted him I would end up getting a load of abuse from him. I could always tell when he was on a high about his betting. He would be transfixed by Teletext all day and would just switch off to everything else.

But for all Paul's bad points, one thing never happened – he never neglected the kids. He may be short-tempered more often than not, but it has always been with me, never with the kids. He adored them; he's always been a great dad, through the bad times and even through the worst times. Perhaps that's why he had such a hold on me. The kids loved him and it would have broken my heart to have deprived the kids of their dad. Believe me, if he had been a really bad dad to those kids I would have walked right out of this house. Everything conspired to build up the pressure on me; I was the one suffering, but for the benefit of the outside world I was suffering in silence. But it's true that you always hurt the one you love. Yes, that was me. I would be the only one to suffer from all Paul's problems. Everything would be my fault; even when he lost his money, it always seemed to be me he would take it out on.

I've now discovered that he had an addictive nature and that there was no way I could have stopped him, no matter what I did. Paul never got a buzz from winning; he got his kicks from having the bet on and waiting for the result. He'd get up in the morning and the only thing on his mind would be placing a bet, and wondering what to put his money on. Once he'd placed the bet he could get on with his day. That was the routine seven days a week for the last year – every single day, day in and day out, it would never stop. In the evening, when the kids had gone to bed, I would have to go out just to get away from him and his gambling.

I had a very loving, supportive, caring friend, Elaine, who is my best friend. But in the end I think Elaine and her husband Neil knew things were really bad as I would be around their place every night moaning about Paul. But they showed such support for me. They helped me out a lot. I might have cracked if I hadn't somewhere to run every night with someone to talk to. They have always been great friends and always will be. You don't come across friends like that every day.

In my eyes gambling was the worst of Paul's addictions. He might be stone-cold sober, but he was still unbearable. And a couple of times I threatened to kick him out of the house, although in reality I didn't really mean it – until I'd reached the very end of my tolerance and patience. I was just trying to frighten him by telling him to get out of the house, but it didn't seem to work. But there were times when I sat there thinking, where could I take the kids, where could I live? There were times when I couldn't stand it any longer in the house. If I had made myself homeless, I'd be just another single parent on the housing list waiting for a home. The most practical thing for myself and the kids was to say goodnight to Paul and to go and sleep in the spare room.

What a contrast now. We're in love again, and it's like it was when we first met and lived together. But I cannot pretend that we don't have our problems; of course we do. Paul had one bad day when he broke down in training. He has other, not so brilliant days when he wakes up feeling like shit, but once he has had the chance to chat with his counsellor, his sponsor and his therapists he feels fine and can get on with his day.

I had one bad day, the first day I was left with the three children all on my own. Sam was only three weeks old. I just felt insecure for some reason, and didn't think I would be able to cope on my own.

Paul had gone for therapy to the hospital in Southampton and rang me from there. I told him how I felt and he sounded really worried about me. I told him that we needed to talk, that we had to iron a few things out. This had nothing to do with his problems, but was to do with me and my problems. I was feeling emotionally drained after giving birth to my third son.

The night before, Paul attended a GA meeting and I went with him. It was a great meeting, extremely therapeutic, but it left me feeling very tired. When we got home I offered to drive the baby-sitter home because Paul said he was absolutely shattered. When I got back Paul was lying on the settee in his dressing gown with Sam just waking up. He hadn't offered to feed the baby, but just waited for me to come home. He saw me, and said, 'I'm off to bed, goodnight.' I just thought to myself, you little shit. There I was, I hadn't had a night's sleep in three weeks, trying to stay happy, and he tells me he's shattered. I had to come home after dropping off the baby-sitter and then feed Sam. Well, what about me? I'm entitled to feel tired, too.

When Paul got back from Southampton he knew what was wrong and we had a long chat and he understood. He was very sorry. He realized that he would have to change his ways. Now he's up first thing every morning with the kids; he feeds the baby, makes the bottles. It's part of his change of character, he is prepared to listen and correct anything that he knows is wrong. I've never had a bad day since.

Now I would say Paul is a completely reformed character, a totally new man. He still has a short temper, but he now knows how to control it. He no longer sits around feeling sorry for himself; he gets on with it.

We had a flare-up just before the European Cup Winners' Cup semi-final first leg against Sampdoria. His time was being consumed by football, as the club had a heavy schedule of matches. He wasn't attending his meetings, and I knew how important they were. I told him that I was concerned that he wasn't attending his meetings. He snapped, 'Why don't you go to your fucking meetings.' But I just stayed quiet. After an hour or so he realized what he had said, and he was so sorry about it that he bought me some red roses and showed that he cared, and that he needed to go to a meeting. He went training and that evening went to a meeting.

I don't expect Paul to be perfect. How can I? Everyone has their ups and downs and that includes Paul and myself. But our disagreements are not self-destructive; they help to keep us together, as we are fighting for the same cause. We have now learned to talk about problems and now if there is anything bothering me or Paul we talk about it and put it right.

I know what Paul has gone through, how much he has suffered, and what he is still going through. But I have now accepted life for how great it is and I wouldn't change it for the world.

Every day Paul acknowledges that he is an alcoholic, that he must never take a drink, must not bet, and not take drugs. It is such a relief to know that he has taken positive steps to cure himself. But until he was able to admit to himself that he had problems he would never have been able to discover a cure. But he went through a lot of soul-searching, and anguish. I'm sure he suffered horrendous withdrawal symptoms. He would always tell me he would give up gambling and drinking, but he knew he had no intention of even trying. It wasn't until he had treatment that he realized the depth of his 'disease'.

At last I have discovered the real meaning of a normal life. Will it continue? Will Paul be strong and remain 'clean'? I believe in him now. I believe that he is a transformed man. I never thought I'd be able to love him again, because our relationship had gone wrong. It had turned so sour that I couldn't bear him to touch me, and I didn't want to sleep in the same room, let alone the same bed. He had turned into someone I didn't really know; he was not the man I had married. But now it has all come back, I do love him again. I love him like I first loved him when we first met, if not more. I never believed I could love him again, but it just shows you the real meaning of love.

You couldn't meet a more lovely man. That is Paul Merson today. His attitude about everything in life is so different from what it used to be. He went off to play golf at the crack of dawn for the

Tony Adams testimonial year even though the team had travelled back that night from Genoa after winning the European Cup Winners' Cup semi-final against Sampdoria on penalties, and he rang me at 6.15 p.m. just to see how I was, and to tell me when he'd be back. That never happened in the past. But a little thing like that call made me feel so warm inside, and so loving towards him. He is now a caring husband. He really cares about me and how I feel. Paul takes Charlie to school and picks him up every day. Now, if I picked him up Charlie would ask, 'Where's dad?'

I think Paul now realizes just how lucky he is. It's the old adage – you never know what you've got until you lose it. And Paul came so close to losing just about everything – his football career, his wife and his kids. I never thought there was such a thing as the perfect wife. Now I believe I must be the perfect wife for Paul to suffer like I did and to still be with him. I've told Paul this often enough. Let's face it, who would have put up with him after all the shit I've had to take? He knows he would be doing well to have found someone else to take my place. No one out there would have put up with him. Only me, because I love him so much. Yes, I love him, and I never stopped loving him. Even when he was up to all his tricks, deep down I loved him, but he just made it intolerable for me.

It's such a relief to have a normal life. At the same time I am no longer concerned about what Paul is up to. I trust him implicitly. And my involvement with his meetings and therapy has been so helpful. I cannot live in his shoes, I cannot be with him every minute of the day. If I worried about what he was doing every single minute I would be a nervous wreck. And it wouldn't be of any use, it wouldn't stop him doing what he wanted to do, if he wanted to do it. I have to relax and trust him. And I do. I know as long as he keeps going to his meetings he will be all right, that he has people to help him through any crisis.

I know he will have bad days. But he's only had one or two bad days since he came out of hospital. One day in particular was a very bad day when he got very depressed. He had gone through so much in a short period of time, it was only to be expected that he would have some tough times on the road back. Paul broke down in training one day. He was in a terrible state. He rang his sponsor, he rang his counsellor. After an hour talking on the phone he emerged from his depression. Then he was fine, perfectly OK. They told him to think about how bad he was in comparison with how bad he had been – and it was nothing like it.

Football is a great therapy for Paul. He loves the sport much more now than he ever did. He has far more respect for it. He has a greater appreciation of what football has brought into his life, and how close he came to throwing it all away.

Actually Paul is a very interesting person. Only six or seven months ago he had basically no conversation, didn't really want to talk to me or anybody else. Now you can't stop him talking. He's talking to his counsellor, his sponsor, members of his three different groups, his group from the hospital. He doesn't stop.

He has acquired so much knowledge about addictions, about himself, about other people's problems, that I wouldn't be surprised if in ten years' time he became a counsellor himself – provided, of course, that he stays 'clean'. And there is no reason to suppose that he won't. Probably most people will think that once he stops playing, once that motivation to stay 'clean' has disappeared because of his livelihood, once he has more time on his hands, that he will go back to his old ways. I don't see that happening. Perhaps I am deluding myself, but I don't think I am.

I have never been this happy, and of course I don't want anything to spoil this happiness. I have so much love for Paul, I never want to let him go, ever. He means so much to me, and I know how much he cares for me.

UPDATE – THE 1995/6 SEASON

Let's start on a positive note. An entire year as an ever-present. A first. And I feel proud of that record. From the time I got back into the Arsenal team I went a complete year without missing a game, a record that was once well beyond my capabilities. Throughout all the years I've been in the game, this is the first season I have played every single game – it's just brilliant! Why has it happened? Well, the answer is simple: it's down to sorting myself out, which has resulted in a higher level of fitness and consistency in my play. As a result I earned a new contract, and gained a wonderful sense of achievement. On a personal level it has been a marvellous season.

However, I have suffered a couple of real downers.

Roger Stanislaus was sacked by Third Division Leyton Orient five days after being banned from football for twelve months by the FA for taking a performance-enhancing drug. Stanislaus, a twenty-seven-year-old defender, was caught out after a routine drugs test following a match against Barnet in November. He faces a huge battle to relaunch his career after the Orient board's unanimous decision to sack him. Barry Hearn, the Orient chairman, said he felt that the one-year ban was a lenient decision, and that the board had no alternative to dismissal in order to preserve the good name of Orient and of football in general.

No one knew how much all that affected me at the time – because Roger was such a close friend during our days together in the Arsenal youth team. He was a year younger than me, but we played in the same team and we were great mates. We toured together and I was gutted for him. But I knew what he was going through. I knew that if he was addicted, it was an illness and he needed help.

But Roger's problems were not the only reminder I needed that I had to fight my own problems day after day without any let-up. One of my close friends who I meet in therapy relapsed, and badly. I felt terrible when I discovered that he was back on the heroin, that he couldn't stop himself. It was a sickening reminder that you cannot take this lightly, a frightening reminder of what faces you every day. Going back on heroin is scary, to say the least. He went through hell again – but the good news was that he was recovering in therapy.

If ever anything can concentrate your mind it is news like that. It illustrates that what lies ahead for me is down to me. It also shows me how lucky I am.

It is those thoughts that get me through some of the problems – even the seemingly insignificant, small ones – that might occur on the pitch. The fans probably wouldn't even notice the sort of thing in a match, or indeed off the field, that can prey on a footballer's mind. Fortunately there haven't been too many of those for me.

The game's ruling body is concentrating its efforts to curb drug-taking in the sport, but I still feel the real evils of the game are drinking and betting. Those problems are far more widespread than drug-taking. Keith Gillespie's problems with betting came to light, but there are many other players hooked on gambling. My advice to them is to realize that gambling is a mug's game, and stop while you can – get some expert advice, and don't be ashamed to do it. Take it from an old gambler . . . How much money can you win? How much money do you need? Do you think you can win more money than you earn? Of course not. You earn enough to buy steak and chips every day if you want, live in a nice house, buy smart clothes, and have a wonderful lifestyle. So why want more? But I understand why players turn to gambling. It's to alleviate boredom, and in many cases a quick cure for depression. Depression and boredom can be brought on by an injury, even a minor one, let alone a career-threatening one. I've been on the top, then all of a sudden, without any warning, I've been on the floor worried sick about an injury, anxious about the future after losing form and being left out of the team. A professional gambler might expect to make a profit out of gambling, but not the poor punter, not the young footballer trying to forget his troubles.

When I read about Keith Gillespie's plight I really felt for him. I am sure there will be many who read about his troubles and thought, what an idiot. That was not my view. I thought, what a shame. It sounded just like me ten years ago. Now that's got to be a warning for the Newcastle winger, it's got to be a warning for anyone in his position. No one wants to go down my route! I have been in his position a thousand times in the past, trying to get out of debt by ploughing more money into bets. It only gets worse, not better. Then comes the slippery slope.

There are many factors behind the reasons players gamble their money, and in some cases their lives, away. It's bad enough when you are out of the team, but the worst thing for a player is the worry over an injury. Many players can cope. It doesn't follow that if you are left out of the team or sidelined through injury for any length of time you will become an alcoholic. Of course not. But young players can become susceptible to depression, and vulnerable if they turn to drink or gambling. The most serious problem arises if a player already has a habit of either gambling or drinking, and then finds himself out of the team and his world collapsing around him as a result of injury. Then the gambling and drinking take a real grip. Then he can become addicted.

Darren Anderton has been injured for most of this season. You can imagine what he has been going through. One minute he is the top man with England, guaranteed a place in the European Championship team, with Terry Venables building the attack around him. The next minute he cannot even play a reserve game. How can you not feel sorry for him? Alan Shearer suffered a long period out of the game, with doubts about his future. That must be one of the worst times of your life: all the self-doubts, all the worries over whether you will ever be the same player. Even if you've got a twisted ankle, it might keep you out for three weeks, or even longer, and the worries are still there. And then you might suffer a number of set-backs, like those that have beset Darren Anderton and indeed Paul Gascoigne.

But not all players need a crutch. It must be difficult, but not all players turn to drink or to gambling for comfort. They battle through the hard way, and they come through it. Many times they come out of their depression with better qualities than before.

Even now I am not free of self-doubts and bouts of depression. I have had a few occasions when such feelings have recurred. One was losing against Tottenham! There have been moments like that, but I have generally managed to get over them quickly enough.

There was only one day when I was really in deep personal trauma. This was by far my worst time – the night we drew 2-2 against Aston Villa in the first leg of the Coca Cola Cup Final at Highbury, after being two goals up.

There it was, the dream of a Wembley appearance, after all I had been through, and just a year after all my troubles. It would have been a marvellous achievement, not just for me, but for the whole team, who all wanted desperately to get to Wembley in Bruce Rioch's first season as manager. Yet for me it would have been extra special, would have meant that all the nightmares, all the sacrifices, all the heartache had been worthwhile.

But I ballsed it up!

Dennis Berkgamp had scored two world-class goals and Wembley was beckoning. Then I made such a terrible mistake. I was back in my own penalty area and tried to head the ball away. I had been playing with such confidence that I thought I could execute a clearance. But it went horribly wrong, the ball ended up bouncing around the area, and then Dwight Yorke scored and put Villa back in the game. It was a silly header and I felt the anguish of blame. No one else blamed me, I blamed myself.

I felt dreadful. I needed the resolve of everything I had learned in over a year of counselling and rehabilitation. Fortunately Lorraine was there at the match, and together we went straight home.

But the temptation to drown my sorrows in drink was immense. I felt so low I felt a draw like a magnet towards alcohol. My head was full of bad, negative thoughts. I recalled all I had gone through over the past year, and reproached myself that in spite of it all I had still made a complete balls-up of it on the pitch. I felt I had let my team-mates down, and let myself down.

I suppose I had come to the stage where after a long, gruelling season, Wembley was so close: there was tangible proof of what I had gone through, there was real hope of some reward for all my sacrifices. I knew it was selfish, but I couldn't help it.

It did not take long to shake myself out of that way of thinking. But it can take just seconds to have that one drink and start all over again.

I could not have got through that moment alone. But with Lorraine's strength and support I got home and called my counsellor, and I talked things over with both him and Lorraine. I knew I dare not return to drink. I just couldn't do it, no matter how low I was feeling. I could have blown everything, so I had to dig in and find new resolve from within, and beat it. It was a nightmare night – but I did beat it. Lorraine was there for me, and all that I had gone through had been for my family first and then my football. The most important thing was to save my family life, and then if anything good came from my football it would be a bonus. I had to remember how I had been before, and how much I wanted to avoid dropping back into those bad old days. That helped enormously. I had a new life, a far better life, and I did not want to throw it all away. That thought kept me going.

After a day the depression lifted. The realisation came that of course I hadn't intentionally made such a vital mistake. No one had pinned it on me, and I began to get over the feeling that maybe it had cost us the dream of a Wembley appearance. My counsellor said that I was bound to have one or two bad moments when all the self-doubts would return, but he stressed that I should focus on all the good times that have come as a result of my effort.

I know what I am like. It wouldn't have stopped at one drink. I'm compulsive, an addict, so I would have had to down every drink I could find that night, and then it would have snowballed back to betting and drugs. The most natural thing in the world for an alcoholic is to drink and then get drunk; the most natural thing in the world for a compulsive gambler is to have a bet and carry on betting; and the most natural thing, for a drug addict is to turn to drugs. It's simply second nature. A lot of people relapse. Many people out there are convinced that I have relapsed.

I haven't.

However, I must admit that, it's hard. Very hard, at times.

Sometimes I forget. I forget how well I have done, forget all the benefits, forget what I have been through to ensure that I am clean. Those are the most dangerous times. You wonder whether you can bear to go through yet another day of this torment. It goes through your mind just how easy it would be to reach out for a drink and to hell with it all.

There are other times, of course, when I go to bed and congratulate myself on getting through another day without touching a single drop, walking past every betting shop, and not having a thought about drugs. I go to sleep with a little 'well done' to myself.

But I know that I also need to tell myself, 'Watch yourself.' I may be fifteen months down the line, but it doesn't get any easier. Every day it's the same. I must overcome, and I can only do that with expert help and caring help. I must keep going to my meetings, I must keep taking my 'medicine'. The experts understand that it is impossible to keep appreciating how well I am doing, every single day. Sometimes it is frightening to realise just how much I have done, and to remind myself that I dare not throw it all away. Sometimes it can become harder, rather than easier, with the passage of time. It means I must never get complacent. I do, of course. But I mustn't. And, I know I mustn't.

So, what would have happened had I gone out for a drink after that semi-final game? Do you think I would have got away with a drinking session? I would have to have found an underground bunker with no one in it! If I am ever caught out with a drink in my hand it will be front-page news! In a way that's a safety-valve, the fear of discovery and the consequences.

It doesn't stop the rumours, of course. There have been plenty of them. Some people have been putting it about that I have been spotted out at this pub or that pub, at this nightclub or that one, naturally with a drink in my hand and looking the worse for wear after more than a couple. You can imagine the score. 'There's Paul at such-and-such a place with his boozy mates, looking paralytic.' How hurtful can people get? Yes, it does hurt when I hear about these rumours. They come from jealous people. Spiteful people. It doesn't surprise me that I am an easy target. But it doesn't make it any less hurtful. Fortunately these lies have not been reported to the manager Bruce Rioch, or if they have been, he has not called me in to answer them. I am glad of that. It shows that he has faith in me.

God forbid that it should happen because I know it would be the end for me if it did. One drink is all it would take and that would be it. I would never be able to stop, and I would be thrown out of the game. I would not expect another chance from the FA.

However, I believe in myself now. I believe that I won't relapse. And, to prove it, there is a special clause in my new contract. If I go back to my wild days the club have the option of tearing up the contract and throwing it in the bin – where it would certainly deserve to go. The contract stipulates that I would lose every bonus and advantage of the new deal awarded to me, including my pay rise. Now, I am sure everyone will say that it was the club which insisted on such a clause to safeguard their own interests. Not at all! I asked for it. I wanted that in my new contract. If I did go off the rails, then I would never kick another football again. Also, I would lose my wife and kids and that is far more important to me.

There is another scenario where I would never kick a ball again – the day I stop enjoying my football. The enjoyment died for me just before I confessed to all my troubles, and then I was ready, and indeed willing, to pack it all in. Luckily I have rekindled my love for the game. I am enjoying my football more than at any time in my entire career. The fans have a lot to do with that. Their reaction to me when I went out at Highbury for the AC Milan game gave me the moral support I needed to carry on. I couldn't face playing again had they booed me. If they turned on me even now, I would find it hard, if not impossible to take. I would pack it in.

I certainly don't count one or two idiots having a pop at me on the pitch at Villa Park at end of the Coca Cola Cup semi-final second leg, as the true feelings of Arsenal fans.

Despite the nightmare of the first leg on a personal level, and the dramatic after-affects, it had long since passed by the time the second leg came around a fortnight later. I was in the right frame of mind for the second leg at Villa Park. In fact, I was determined to put things right. We played well, had plenty of chances, but did everything except get the goal that would have taken us to Wembley.

It wasn't a particularly savoury end to our cup run with the fans running onto the pitch at the end of the match. I went over to clap our fans for the backing they'd given us and there were just a couple of fans shouting abuse at me.

Everybody else was brilliant, no problems. The fans could see for themselves that we were unlucky not to get to Wembley and that we had given it our all. If this had happened after we had gone out of the FA Cup at Sheffield United I could have understood a little more. But not this time. We deserved to win.

I want to make it clear that I had no problems with the majority of Arsenal fans. I went over to our supporters to applaud them and there was this one guy screaming, shouting and waving his arms at me. He was giving me abuse and we made eye contact. I had a go back at him and some of the things I said were unprintable. But I can tell you some of the things he said to me are also unprintable. I think it just took me by surprise. I am used to getting stick from away supporters and most of the time you cannot hear what is said anyway. But this was the first time I had ever had it from someone in Arsenal's colours. At the end of a bad night, I just reacted. I was upset at missing out on Wembley. But I was wrong and I'm sorry. As it turned out he too realised he was out of order. The fan faxed me an apology the very next day. He sent a fax to the club and followed it up with a letter. I don't hold any grudge against the fans. After all they spend their money and they are entitled to their opinions. I respect that. But there are decent ways of showing it.

The pitch invasion was worrying because fans are running straight at you. You don't know if they want to pat you on the back or have a go at you. They were all friendly, but it does seem to happen at Villa a lot.

'Wrightie' was caught up in the celebrations by the Villa fans but I didn't know until afterwards that he had experienced some aggro too.

Moving away from the negative aspects of our game, everyone is asking me how Arsenal will do in the future. Can we become as big a force in the game as we used to be?

I am convinced that Bruce Rioch will build one of the most powerful squads in the country, but it won't be easy. The competition has never been tougher. Newcastle, Manchester United and Liverpool have constructed formidable sides at enormous cost. Robbie Fowler is a great player, and I voted for him as the Young Player of the Year . . . as a former Young Player of the Year winner myself! I voted for Les Ferdinand and he won the senior award. In fact, I had a suspicion that Fowler might have won both awards, just like Andy Gray some years back. Les got my vote for all the great goals he scored. It was between him and Alan Shearer as far as I was concerned. My vote goes to the best player, not because he's a nice bloke, or whether he talks to me or not! But as it happens, Les is a nice bloke. Fowler is a great goal-scorer, but I am not quite so sure he is going to be one of the best of all time as some people seem to think.

In the voting you cannot choose a player from your own club, otherwise Dennis Bergkamp would have got my vote. In Dennis we have the best player I have ever played with by far. His attitude and skill are of the highest level. He is always the last player to leave the training pitch. No matter how hard you work, you can't work as hard as Dennis. He's always out there with Bruce Rioch, or he might be on his own, just doing a bit extra, working on his technique, trying something different. He's unbelievable – the best player at the club and the hardest grafter. I am the first to admit that it's not easy to get to the top and it's even harder staying there. I got there, thought I knew it all and decided I didn't have to train, didn't have to listen. Looking at Dennis shows how it should be done.

David Platt, one of our key signings, was out of the side for much of the season through injury. For that reason he hasn't been able to impose his considerable ability within the structure of the side. But I am sure he will make a big impact when he is fully fit next season.

I am sure there will be further key signings for next season and that we shall be a major force under Bruce Rioch. Everyone talks about all the players he should sell and buy. And I have no doubt that he has been chasing quite a few of those who have been mentioned.

I keep on hearing that our defence is getting old and needs replacing. But they seem as solid as ever to me. We are also changing our style under the new manager. We play a 3-5-1-2, similar to the Liverpool formation. The manager has switched to a three centre half formation and I am sure that is how we shall start the new season.

Everyone wants to know what the new manager is really like. There seem to be so many rumours about his relationship with the players. But the majority of the incidents I read in the papers don't seem to have any resemblance to what actually goes on behind the scenes in the dressing room and on the training pitch. His reputation as a confrontational manager is totally unjustified. Personally I cannot speak highly enough of our new manager. I have been lucky enough to have played under two great managers at Arsenal – George Graham and now Bruce Rioch. Rioch gives me unbelievable confidence in myself. He has tried me in a new role, a sort of floating role with Dennis Bergkamp, with the license to go where the space materialises. It is a position that suits me, and the rest of the players think it is my best position. If I keep playing well I am sure he will keep me in that role.

A week before we reported for training I met him and he took the trouble to find out first hand about my addictions. He promised that he would look after me, and he has been as good as his word. He must have confidence in me because I have played every game since he became boss. He has listened to me during the course of the season. If I report to the training ground feeling less than one hundred per cent he can understand why. It gives me the confidence to confide in him if at any time I am feeling down. He has given me a new contract, an additional year, which means I now have two more seasons left on my current contract, which takes me up to the age of thirty.

This has been my Testimonial Year and taking everything into consideration it has been a milestone season for me. I was thrilled that six hundred people turned up at the Royal Lancaster Hotel for my testimonial dinner. Sometimes those sort of evenings are hard for me, and I tend to stay away from such social occasions for obvious reasons – everyone likes a drink, and who can blame them? But this was a night I enjoyed.

Now I drink Lucozade. That's my favourite drink. I'm just the most boring footballer in the world! That's what people say about me – but they are only joking. They say I'm boring because

197

I don't drink, don't smoke, don't gamble, and don't take drugs. But life is just fantastic and if that means I'm boring, then so be it. Lorraine and I have never been so close, and my relationship with my kids is brilliant.

The happiness of my family is the most important issue in my life, because I have been close to finishing with football. If the fans had not backed me that night when I came on as a substitute against AC Milan, I would have walked off that Highbury pitch for the very last time. I know that now, and I probably knew it then. I suppose everyone thought that the fans would have given me a good reception because I am one of them. But I had been a bad boy and they could easily have turned against me. I would have understood. No-one would have blamed them. But the fans were on my side, they gave me the sort of cheer I wanted, the kind of reception I didn't really deserve. They gave me the strength to carry on playing, and they continue to do that.

Now I feel that my career can be prolonged by quite a few years. I've never felt fitter or more committed and I am still only twenty-eight.

The ambition is still there, and I'm convinced that next season the Arsenal will again be one of the most powerful clubs in the country. My ambition is to win the League again. The Championship is THE trophy. Forget what they tell you about the glamour of the FA Cup. I'd rather win one Premiership title than two FA Cups. The league is the ultimate prize.